The adventures of a bank-note. In two volumes. Volume 3 of 4

Thomas Bridges

ECCO
PRINT EDITIONS

Eighteenth Century
Collections Online
Print Editions

Gale ECCO Print Editions

Relive history with *Eighteenth Century Collections Online*, now available in print for the independent historian and collector. This series includes the most significant English-language and foreign-language works printed in Great Britain during the eighteenth century, and is organized in seven different subject areas including literature and language; medicine, science, and technology; and religion and philosophy. The collection also includes thousands of important works from the Americas.

The eighteenth century has been called "The Age of Enlightenment." It was a period of rapid advance in print culture and publishing, in world exploration, and in the rapid growth of science and technology – all of which had a profound impact on the political and cultural landscape. At the end of the century the American Revolution, French Revolution and Industrial Revolution, perhaps three of the most significant events in modern history, set in motion developments that eventually dominated world political, economic, and social life.

In a groundbreaking effort, Gale initiated a revolution of its own: digitization of epic proportions to preserve these invaluable works in the largest online archive of its kind. Contributions from major world libraries constitute over 175,000 original printed works. Scanned images of the actual pages, rather than transcriptions, recreate the works *as they first appeared.*

Now for the first time, these high-quality digital scans of original works are available via print-on-demand, making them readily accessible to libraries, students, independent scholars, and readers of all ages.

For our initial release we have created seven robust collections to form one the world's most comprehensive catalogs of 18th century works.

Initial Gale ECCO Print Editions collections include:

History and Geography
Rich in titles on English life and social history, this collection spans the world as it was known to eighteenth-century historians and explorers. Titles include a wealth of travel accounts and diaries, histories of nations from throughout the world, and maps and charts of a world that was still being discovered. Students of the War of American Independence will find fascinating accounts from the British side of conflict.

Social Science

Delve into what it was like to live during the eighteenth century by reading the first-hand accounts of everyday people, including city dwellers and farmers, businessmen and bankers, artisans and merchants, artists and their patrons, politicians and their constituents. Original texts make the American, French, and Industrial revolutions vividly contemporary.

Medicine, Science and Technology

Medical theory and practice of the 1700s developed rapidly, as is evidenced by the extensive collection, which includes descriptions of diseases, their conditions, and treatments. Books on science and technology, agriculture, military technology, natural philosophy, even cookbooks, are all contained here.

Literature and Language

Western literary study flows out of eighteenth-century works by Alexander Pope, Daniel Defoe, Henry Fielding, Frances Burney, Denis Diderot, Johann Gottfried Herder, Johann Wolfgang von Goethe, and others. Experience the birth of the modern novel, or compare the development of language using dictionaries and grammar discourses.

Religion and Philosophy

The Age of Enlightenment profoundly enriched religious and philosophical understanding and continues to influence present-day thinking. Works collected here include masterpieces by David Hume, Immanuel Kant, and Jean-Jacques Rousseau, as well as religious sermons and moral debates on the issues of the day, such as the slave trade. The Age of Reason saw conflict between Protestantism and Catholicism transformed into one between faith and logic -- a debate that continues in the twenty-first century.

Law and Reference

This collection reveals the history of English common law and Empire law in a vastly changing world of British expansion. Dominating the legal field is the *Commentaries of the Law of England* by Sir William Blackstone, which first appeared in 1765. Reference works such as almanacs and catalogues continue to educate us by revealing the day-to-day workings of society.

Fine Arts

The eighteenth-century fascination with Greek and Roman antiquity followed the systematic excavation of the ruins at Pompeii and Herculaneum in southern Italy; and after 1750 a neoclassical style dominated all artistic fields. The titles here trace developments in mostly English-language works on painting, sculpture, architecture, music, theater, and other disciplines. Instructional works on musical instruments, catalogs of art objects, comic operas, and more are also included.

The BiblioLife Network

This project was made possible in part by the BiblioLife Network (BLN), a project aimed at addressing some of the huge challenges facing book preservationists around the world. The BLN includes libraries, library networks, archives, subject matter experts, online communities and library service providers. We believe every book ever published should be available as a high-quality print reproduction; printed on-demand anywhere in the world. This insures the ongoing accessibility of the content and helps generate sustainable revenue for the libraries and organizations that work to preserve these important materials.

The following book is in the "public domain" and represents an authentic reproduction of the text as printed by the original publisher. While we have attempted to accurately maintain the integrity of the original work, there are sometimes problems with the original work or the micro-film from which the books were digitized. This can result in minor errors in reproduction. Possible imperfections include missing and blurred pages, poor pictures, markings and other reproduction issues beyond our control. Because this work is culturally important, we have made it available as part of our commitment to protecting, preserving, and promoting the world's literature.

GUIDE TO FOLD-OUTS MAPS and OVERSIZED IMAGES

The book you are reading was digitized from microfilm captured over the past thirty to forty years. Years after the creation of the original microfilm, the book was converted to digital files and made available in an online database.

In an online database, page images do not need to conform to the size restrictions found in a printed book. When converting these images back into a printed bound book, the page sizes are standardized in ways that maintain the detail of the original. For large images, such as fold-out maps, the original page image is split into two or more pages

Guidelines used to determine how to split the page image follows:

• Some images are split vertically; large images require vertical and horizontal splits.
• For horizontal splits, the content is split left to right.
• For vertical splits, the content is split from top to bottom.
• For both vertical and horizontal splits, the image is processed from top left to bottom right.

THE

ADVENTURES

OF A

BANK - NOTE.

VOL. III.

THE

ADVENTURES

OF A

BANK-NOTE.

IN FOUR VOLUMES.

VOL. III.

——*Explebo numerum, reddarque tenebris.*
VIRG. ÆN.

When I've held up a proper number
Of fools and knaves, and fuch-like lumber,
To public view, and public fcorn,
Contented I'll to duft return.

LONDON,

Printed fol T. DAVIES, in Ruffel-ftreet,
Covent-garden. 1771.

THE

ADVENTURES

OF A

BANK-NOTE.

CHAP. I.

A short dissertation on light reading.

BEFORE I finished my second volume, I brought the poor curate fairly out of his troubles, and defy any of my readers to say I left the parson in the suds; on the contrary, I left him happy with his twenty pounds in his pocket to pay his whole debts with, which amounted to little more than half his capital.—

How happy would three fourths of ..t- ders in coaches, chariots, vis-a-vees, whiſkeys, curricles, &c. &c. &c. &c. be, if they could ſay half as much; but as that is not to be ex-pected, we will e'en leave them to ride further and further into debt, till they whirl to the gates of a pa-lace cālled the King's-Bench, or ſome other of his majeſty's build-ings, fitted up with needleſs iron bars to keep people in, that can't keep themſelves out.

In the firſt part of my firſt and ſecond volumes I proceeded to tell you, in a regular manner, how I walked out of one perſon's pocket into another; and deſigned to have done ſo to the end of about twenty volumes, which is as much as I ex-pect

pect to fill; but fince my jumł .
with the printer and his devil obliged
me to pop in my ftories juft as I
could recollect them, you muft not
expect any more regularity from me:
fuch a head as mine once put wrong,
is not eafily put to rights again ; if
therefore I tell you into whofe hands
I fell, that is all you muft now look
for ; but which way, or how, or
when, or why, or wherefore, if you
expect any account, ten to one you
will be difappointed.

I fell by good luck into the hands
of a gentleman of fortune and family, with whofe company I was fo
much pleafed, that I wifhed to fpend
all the days of my flender life with
him ; but as the good old women
fay, if wifhes were horfes, who would

walk afoot ? Would you, Mr. Circu-
lator of greafy volumes ? To you I ad-
drefs myfelf, becaufe I know you will
do me the honour to read the firft half
dozen pages, to enable you to give
your opinion to your good cuftomers, the youg ladies, and milleners
apprentices, whether my book is
likely to prove fine light tragical
reading, or one of your heavy merry
books ? I mention your own words
in this defcription of books, becaufe I heard you give the beft reafons for your expreffions that ever
man did; and I honour both your
full powdered white wig and yourfelf for it. " Sir," fays you to a gentleman, in whofe pocket I lay, and
who feemed to ftare at the novelty of
your ideas, " I call your very tragical
" books the lighteft reading, becaufe
" they

" they move the nimbleſt from my
" ſhelves. A crying volume, Sir,"
adds you, with an air that would do
honour to the librarian of the Spaniſh
monarch, " brings me more money in
" ſix months than a heavy merry thing
" will do in ſix years : have I not rea-
" ſon, Sir," quoth you, " for what I
" advance ?" " Indeed," ſays the gentleman in whoſe pocket I lay, making
a profound obeiſance either to your
wig, perſon, or underſtanding, but
which I declare I never yet could
learn ; " I muſt own you are perfectly
" right." Upon this you returned the
gentleman's compliment with ſo
ſmirking a ſide-bow, that had your
hands been ſtuck in a muff, I ſhould
have miſtaken you for the inimitable
Mr. Nailem himſelf; but as I have
loſt more time already in talking

with,

with, and about you, than our readers will thank us for, I fhall e'en
proceed to my bufinefs without
waiting for an anfwer; whether you
would not rather chufe to ride than
walk on foot?

Mr. Villiers, for that is the name
of the gentleman into whofe hands I
mentioned I luckily fell, was no
drinker of a bottle after dinner, a
glafs or two fufficed his occafions; he
therefore feldom failed to be at one
coffee-houfe or other nigh the play-
houfes by five o'clock, to fpend an
hour before the play began; by
which means I had an opportunity
of hearing a curious dialogue, now
and then, from people in the next
box, or the next but one or two, or
even at the other end of the room;
for

for my organs of hearing are excellent. One evening when Mr. Villiers was busy in perusing a paper of punch — Now did I foresee I should be interrupted by that there fellow with the flat nose, who is snuffling out, " What the devil is a paper of " punch ?" Why, you Dutch mastiff-faced hobgobblin, if your brains had not been as much compressed against the back part of your skull, as your nose is against the fore part, you would soon have conceived that a paper of punch is a paper of contradictions, which all our news papers are : do not all the nations in the world, the Hottentots not excepted, call a bowl of punch a bowl of English contradictions ? and if bitter, and sweet, and sour, and strong, and small, mixt all together are not contradic-

B 4   tions,

tions, then your nose is no contradic-
tion to Hogarth's line of beauty; so
pray keep your ignorance to yourself,
and do not interrupt me and my
sensible readers any more.

C H A P. II.

*The great advantage of a Justice of
Peace knowing the world before he
studies Burn.*

I Wish that fellow with the flat
nose had minded his own business, and been poisoning all the
neighbours by vending stinking tal-
low, instead of interrupting me: he
has broke the thread of my discourse;
and as I never learnt to make a true
weaver's knot, I shall hardly be able

to

to tye it neatly together again : but I will do my beſt ; and the Engliſh are naturally ſuch good-natured ſouls, that when they ſee a man doing his utmoſt to pleaſe, they always take the will for the deed ; therefore the moment I can recollect where that otter-faced fellow put me out, I will go on.

I have it now—the landlady is bawling out, " Carry that twelve penny- " worth of punch to Doctor Plump- " cheeks." The word punch has made me recollect I left off at a paper of punch. But before I proceed, I cannot for the ſoul of me help aſking, why you never ſee a parſon call for leſs than twelve-penny worth, when few laymen exceed ſix-penny worth, though perhaps they may repeat it oftener ? But not to treſpaſs on your

patience,

patience, gentle reader, I will proceed in my tale, and call to-morrow for an anſwer to my queſtion.

As Mr. Villiers was reading this paper of punch, written or printed by a Mr. Say, who, on one ſide of the leaf tells you that the Ruſſians had killed fifty thouſand Turks; and on the other ſide the leaf ſays, that the plague had deſtroyed this fifty thouſand Turks three days before the battle. Whilſt Mr. Villiers, I ſay, was peruſing this curious paper, I was liſtening to as curious a dialogue in the next box, between a Jamaica planter, and a young lieutenant of the navy, who I found was his rela-lation———" Jack," ſays the planter, " have you ſeen my couſin, your " grand-father, ſince you came " home ?" Yes," ſays Jack, " I left

" him

" him but yesterday." " Did he re-
" ceive you as usual," says his, friend.
" Better than usual," replies this
Jack Pickle; " I have the witnesses
" in my pocket," saying this, he
pulled out a handful of guineas;
" Hey day ! from whence came
" these singing birds, Jack ?" says
the kinsman. " I will tell you,"
returns Jack. " You shall have the
" whole voyage from my outset to
" mooring in this birth. I went
" passenger in the Bigglefwade cat,
" and took shipping at the Crofs-
" Keys, in Gracechurch-Street; we
" run down before the wind at about
" five knots an hour; and were
" twice very near being overset,
" though the gale was moderate, but
" then the bulk of our loading was
" above deck : however, we arrived
" at last safe at Bigglefwade; I and
" an-

" another only put afhore there, the
" reft proceeded on their voyage to
" York. I foon reached my grand-
" father's cabbin, who was fpecial
" glad to fee me, and foon ftowed
" my after-hold full of roaft beef.
" We then had a good deal of jaw
" together; and he told me a long
" rigmaroll of things that happened
" the year after the queen of Sheba
" took a trip to vifit king Solomon.
" I foon found the old gentleman
" was beft pleafed when I laughed
" heartily, fo I had nought to do
" but let him go on, and I kept
" laughing, without minding a fin-
" gle word he faid. At laft fome-
" thing put it into his head to fpeak
" about my father's fudden death,
" which fet the old man a-crying.
" I not knowing but he was going on
" with his bag of tales, kept laughing

" on

" on ſtill : " What, ſirrah, (ſays the
" old gentleman) are you ſuch a pro-
" fligate as to laugh at your father's
" death?" Death! (ſays I, rather ſur-
" priſed to find myſelf runnıng bump
" upon a lee-ſhore, and how to tack
" about ſuddenly was the difficulty ;)
" death¹ grandfather? (ſays I) " Yes,
" ſirrah, (ſays he) I was lamenting
" your father's death, and you fell
" a-laughing." By this time I had fill-
" ed the foreſail, and calling to my-
" ſelf, Helm a lee, got upon the other
" tack in the twinkling of a marling-
" ſpike. Lord, grandfather (ſays I)
" I was ſo buſy in thinking of that
" laſt merry ſtory, that I could not
" help laughing over again, ſo loſt
" what you ſaid about my poor fa-
" ther. This ſet all to rights, and
" we ſoon got under way again.

" The

" The day that I came away after
" we had dined, and the old gentle-
" man had gotten his pipe ftuck into
" his jaws, and was beginning fome
" of his old ftories, part of which he
" made, and dreamt the reft : I hap-
" pened to fay, Lord, grândfather,
" you muft have read a great deal,
" and ftudied very hard to know all
" you do."

C H A P. III.

The Juftice continued.

" GRandfon, (fays the juftice) I
" ftudy nothing but the law
" now: in my youth, when I had
" little notion of being fo ufeful to
" my country as I am at prefent,
" I was

" I was a great reader of ſtory-
" books, and knew a merry book
" as well as any body. Our parſon,
" who I never thought a great ſcho-
" lar, uſed to commend a merry
" book he called John Quickſets and
" Sanchleys Pancakes, and would have
" lent me the books, but as every
" pariſh has ſome clever fellow at
" quickſets, and ſome good houſewife
" to fry pancakes, I did not think
" it worth while to borrow his book.
" The parſon in the main is an honeſt
" ſoul; in every thing but books
" we agree very well, for I never
" knew him flinch from a bottle or
" pipe. Now the books I uſed to
" read I remember had ſome life
" and ſoul in them; there was Ro-
" binſon Cruſoe and his Man Fri-
" day, two fine fellows; then there

was

" was the hiſtory of Captain What-
" d'y-call-um, that was ſhipwrecked
" upon an uninhabited iſland in the
" deſerts of Arabia; then there is
" the hiſtory of the Pirates in the
" Weſtern Indies—what a glorious
" fellow that Captain Blackbeard
" was! he ſhot two mutineers with
" his own hands for refuſing to eat
" ſalt with their dumplings. I did
" not read that part myſelf, but I
" heard my landlady at the Shoul-
" der of Mutton ſay it is ſo in her
" book." Bleſs me, grandfather,
" ſays I, what with converſation,
" and what with reading, what a
" fund or knowledge you have laid
" in ! " Knowledge, my boy! aye,
" aye, not only of land matters, but
" of ſhip matters too. I have ſtole
" ſo much knowledge by talking
" with

" with my brother, the admiral, that
" I think I could carry a ſhip thro'
" the Baltick into the Mediterranean
" almoſt as ſoon as himſelf." Aye,
" and ſooner too, I'll anſwer for it,
" ſays I, with a little practice. " A
" little practice! boy; aye, and a
" very little practice too, would have
" carried me round the world better
" than admiral Anſon. I would not
" have ſtuck upon the Cape's Horns
" ſo many months, ſtarving and
" freezing, as he did, I'll warrant
" you, boy; though I think people
" made more noiſe about getting
" over them Horns than they need
" have done. "You are right, ſays
I, " but he did it to make folks
" think him a very clever fellow:
" he knew on which ſide his bread
" was buttered. But you ſeem to
Vol. III. C " know

" know all the world, grandfather.
" Pray, how could you get fo much
" knowledge by your own fire-fide,
" as I may fay ? " Knowledge ! my
" boy," fays the old fellow, his dim
" eyes twinkling with pleafure all
" the time, " why, I have not told
" you half yet; I know there is a
" great prolific fea called the At-
" lambftick, that the Spaniards have
" almoft all to themfelves : then
" there is the Laplanders, that inha-
" bit the coaft of Portugal; then
" there is your Greenland whales, and
" white bears, from the emprefs of
" Morocco's dominions; then there
" is Ruffia leather, and olives, from
" Pen'ylvania; then there is your
" Turks, and your Tartars, and
" fugar planters, all along the gold
" coaft in Canada; then there is your
" ele-

" elephants, and crocodiles, in the
" river Nile in Jamaica: in fhort,
" boy, a man would hardly be able
" to tell all I know in a week." Nor
" in a month neither, at the rate you
" go on, grandfather, fays I.   I
" expect I fhall never know fo much
" as long as I live, if I was to keep
" a reckoning for the whole fhip's
" company, mafter, and mate, and
" all. " May be not," fays the juf-
" tice ; " every body was not born
" with fuch a memory to reftrain
" things, when they have catched
" them, as me : but have a good
" heart, my boy; a relation of mine
" can never want fenfe enough to
" get through this world." At
" thefe words he rofe up, and went
" to his defk, and fell to counting
" his money, to know what he could

" fpare

" spare for his annual present. Five
" guineas used to be the sum : but
" the fund of knowledge I had
" found in him, I did not fear would
" help me to something more; nor was
" I disappointed, for he brought me
" twenty guineas; told me I was a
" fine boy, and as I was partly a man
" now, he did not doubt but I
" knew how to manage my money.
" On this I pocketed the cash along
" with his blessing, and away I
" luffed. I could not help, as I
" plied up to Bigglefwade, to get
" into the track of the York Fly-
" boat, from being pleased at leav-
" ing the good old man so well con-
" tented with himself. Although
" he had turned the world, that
" poor I was to get through, quite
" upside down ; and had so jumbled
" the

" the Turks, and Tartars, with the
" fugar planters, and Greenland
" whales, that it will be a difficult
" matter foon to know which is
" which ; but as you are my friend,
" I am glad he has landed you all
" fafe upon the gold coaft in Cana-
" da. I began to be afraid that in
" complaifance to the bulk of your
" companions, the whales, he would
" have left you to raife fugars either
" in the North Sea, or the Bay of
" Bifcay ; in both which places the
" foil would have been too wet for
" you ; but on fecond thoughts I
" found he could not in juftice land
" you any where but where he did,
" becaufe he directly fent a troop of
" elephants to Jamaica, to trample
" down your plantations, to which
" he added an army of crocodiles to

C 3   " eat

" eat up all your negroes : but in
" the main he is a good old foul,
" Ned, and, I will anfwer for him,
" did not know he was doing fo much
" mifchief ; therefore I hope you will
" forgive him, and not think the
" worfe of him." " My thoughts of
" him," fays the kinfman of this Jack
Pickle, very gravely, " I fhall keep
" to myfelf ; but I fhall tell you
" what I think of you, if you de-
" fire it." " I do defire it," fays
Pickle. "Then," adds his companion,
" I agree with your grandfather in
" thinking you not only a fine boy,
" but fo very fine a boy, that you
" would grace a cart up Holborn-
" hill better than any hero that has
" rode that cavalcade thefe twenty
" years." " But not," fays Pickle,
with the greateft good humour in
the

the world, " fo long as my twenty
" guineas laft, which are all fafe yet;
" and to keep them fo I fhall make
" you pay for the coffee;" which the
planter inftantly did, and away
they both went.

Now, if I had a good hand at
thofe matters, what a curious differ-
tation could I write upon the honeft
well-meaning fimplicity of the juftice,
and the archnefs of this pickled
grandfon of his; but, alas, my talent
lays another road. I can recount a
plain fact, without either adding or
diminifhing, and make a fhift to underftand myfelf, though perhaps not
many of my readers can; but as to
differtations, obfervations, allegati-
ons, ratiocinations, elucidations, de-
predations, elevations, atteftations,

C 4 emen-

emendations, deliberations, beatifica-
tions, purgations, sanctifications, eja-
culations, dulcorations, exemplifica-
tions, expectorations, asseverations,
agitations, examinations, perpetra-
tions, annihilations, determinations,
procrastinations, restorations, saliva-
tions, exculpations, circulations, ag-
gravations, animations, renunciations,
anticipations, assassinations, associa-
tions, capitulations, ratifications, cal-
cinations, derivations, participations,
and all the congregations of quota-
tions, or even gratifications, &c. &c.
&c. too tedious for me to recollect,
or my reader to read, I pretend not
to meddle with them at all, but leave
each article to the person best qualified to handle it; only recommend-
ing to the learned doctor A, the re-
verend and thrice learned doctor B;
the

the very learned parſon C, and the ſtill more learned Mr. D, &c. &c. to follow my example, and take particular care they don't fall upon the ſubject they are the leaſt qualified to handle.

Very ingenious men have ſplit upon this rock before now ; and, by miſtaking their talents, have cut as bad a figure as I ſhould do if I attempted to ſpeak in the houſe of commons; let not then the learned doctors, and eſquires, and maſters, to whom I give theſe hints, take it in dudgeon ; I mean them well, and, as a good chriſtian, I ſhould rejoice to ſee their light ſhine before men; but too many of them who have great learning, for want of a little

judg-

judgment, keep burning their candle under a bufhel, and all their life-time, for the guts of them, can neither get the candle out of the bufhel, nor the bufhel kick'd off the candle, by which means many a candle ; which, if properly placed, might have exhibited a ftriking light, has burnt wafte for forty years, and then gone out without its neareft neighbour's knowing it ever exifted ; and this will eternally happen, till our great wifdom fhall think proper to follow that unerring rule ; ftudy firft to know thyfelf, which that you may all do both black coats and brown—from the lawn fleeves to the tattered caffock ; from the curled magnificent phyfical wig, to the thread-bare poet's curl-lefs bri-

gadier,

gadier, is the hearty prayer of, worthy and thrice learned

Sirs,

Your moſt devoted and

Moſt obedient, and moſt

Humble ſervant, and ſincere

Well-wiſher, &c. &c. &c.

C H A P. IV.

A Taylor's ſoul coſts as much ſaving
as a Man's.

THE Jamaica planter and his
hopeful kinſman, the lieutenant, had not been gone five minutes before their box was occupied
by two well looking gentlemen, to
whoſe

whofe difcourfe I prick'd up my ears
directly ; they fat filent till the coffee came, but the moment the fumes
of that vivifying liquor reached their
noftrils, one of them began to fpeak.
" I thought," fays the youngeft "you
" would have been near Uxbridge
" before this." " So I fhould," replies the other, " but my wrong-
" headed pious rogue of a taylor
" has not got my fhooting jacket
" done; my humanity will not fuf-
" fer me to turn the rogue off, on
" account of his family; and yet
" thefe pretended holy vermin have
" gotten fuch hold on the fellow's
" fmall fhare of fenfes, that I fear
" he will be a beggar as long as he
" lives. How do you think he has
" ferved me ?" " I fhould be glad
" to hear," fays the friend. " I'll
" tell

" tell you," rejoins the firſt ſpeaker, who was a fine looking fellow, only his eyes were placed ſo far back in his head, that nature fearing they might not keep ſo good a guard on his face as was neceſſary, had fur- niſhed him with a noſe that jutted out as far as a ſnail's horns, and be- ing as ſenſible to the touch, was of the ſame uſe in giving him notice when he aproached near any danger ; I don't inſinuate by this that he had a tender noſe ; but in the main, that he looked like a man that it would be very dangerous to take by the noſe.

" I called," ſays the owner of the long noſe, " on this pious devil of " a taylor, the day before yeſterday, " and ordered him to get my coat " done,

" done, and bring it home this morn-
" ing." " Sir," says the poor ragged
loufe-feeder, " I would not work
" to-morrow if you would give me
" this world and another such; it
" is a folemn faft day." " Upon my
" word, fays I, I am glad to find our
" bifhops are fo alert, and our great
" men fo religioufly inclined; it is
" a very proper ftep, to be fure, for
" this poor nation is threatened not
" only with war, but the plague like-
" wife, and then famine naturally en-
" fues; therefore on that account I
" think a folemn faft very neceffary."

" That account !" fays this vermin
canibal, " our faft is a faft of our own
" appointing, and on a ten times
" more melancholy account than all
" the plagues and famines in the
" world; what more melancholy ac-
                    " count,

" count," says I, a little alarmed, can possibly happen? " Sir," says the fellow, (stretching his face a-bove a foot and a half long by his own measure, which, tho' a short yard, yet half of it long enough for any Christian's face,) " can you, Sir, " live in this country, and not know " that the thirteenth apostle, the pi-" ous, the devout, the most reve-" rend, and most religious Doctor " Squintum is dead, and the bre-" thren have appointed a solemn fast " on the dreadful occasion? But how " to face the good soul that preaches " the funeral sermon, unless I can " muster a quarter guinea to drop " on the plate, I know not; and I " have but three shillings in the " world to purchase one with." " Why, sirrah," says I, for here I lost

all

all patience, " you dolt, you afs,
" you driveller, you wet-nurfe to
" miriads of black lifted cattle, is
" it not enough that the departed
" fcoundrel robbed you both of your
" money and fenfes whilft he was
" alive, but you muft let one of his
" rogues, at his death, double thofe
" robberies upon you ? Is not this
" quarter guinea to make up a fum
" to pray for the falvation of the
" good man's foul, becaufe he had
" fo many of his flock to take care
" on, that it is fuppofed he had very
" little time to look after his own ?"
" Lord, mafter," fays the fhamble-
knee'd rogue, with his face fhort-
ened half in half,) " I find you are
" one of us, and have been joking
" me all this time ; why, the money
" is for that very ufe : no body could
" know

" know it but one of the elect."
" One of the infane, you mean, fays
" I, you dried fprat.—Here in-
" deed I was tempted, in my paf-
" fion, to call names; but as I had
" talked to him fo cooly before, I
" thought I would keep my temper
" ftill.—Why, you calves head
" without brains, fays I, have
" not I feen you amongft the rab-
" ble, with a mouth wide enough to
" fwallow a common barn-door
" fowl, feathers and all, roaring a-
" gainft popery and flavery; and
" now you fwallow one of the grof-
" eft tenets of popery which the dif-
" guifed Jefuits, your preachers,
" every now and then fuffer un-
" guardedly to appear barefaced, as
" Teague fays, the devil fometimes
" lets his cloven foot. At the men-

Vol. III.　　　D　　　" tion

" tion of the word devil, he opened
" his fhears, and put himfelf in an
" attitude, as if he defigned to fnip
" his head off the inftant he appear-
" ed, although at the fame time I
" could perceive the hair on the
" crown of his head making an ef-
" fort to rife, but was fo loaded with
" animalculæ, that only a few ftrag-
" ling hairs could obey the impulfe,
" and thofe indeed did ftand as erect
" as a front line of grenadiers.
" What the devil is the matter with
" the fellow? fays I, From whence
" comes this look of horror and dif-
" may? " O Sir!" fays the con-
" fumer of cucumbers, " you have
" mentioned the devil twice, and he
" is not a gentleman to be joked
" with, unlefs at the Tabernacle; for
" there our holy teacher can handle
" him

" him as he pleases." Not so well,
" says I, as he can handle your mo-
" ney, you white livered varlet ;
" but what do you give him your
" money for ? " For his trouble in
" saving my precious soul," says
" stitch.—Why, sirrah, says I, for
" now I began, spite of my teeth, to
" be in a real passion, you shal-
" low crowned baboon, you walk-
" ing skeleton, are you fool enough
" to scrape, and cheat, and cabbage,
" all you can lay your hands on, and
" starve your thin-gutted self and
" your whole family, in order to pay
" a better price for your ninth part
" of a soul, than the drunken hosier
" over the way does for a whole soul.
" Let me see you work more on
" week-days, instead of following
" those designing villains ; steal less,

" and

" and employ your earnings entirely
" for the use of your family; thank
" God with a grateful heart, when
" you go to bed, for his blessings:
" this will enable you to go decently
" dressed on a Sunday to your parish
" church, and, with a good consci-
" ence, pay your devotions to your
" Maker, who entrusted every man
" with his own talent, and expects
" an account from himself, and not
" leave his reckoning to a holy attor-
" ney, who will be damned long be-
" fore he can put in an appearance
" for you. This will be the true
" way, not only to save that frac-
" tion of a soul of yours, but to
" give you courage in this world, nei-
" ther to be afraid of the devil, nor
" even mankind, who are several of
" them, I have reason to think, as
" bad,

" bad, if not worfe than the devil
" himfelf: fo fit down, and get my
" coat done, and work to-morrow
" to earn money, inftead of fafting,
" and praying, and running in debt
" to change your three fhillings into
" a quarter-guinea, to fave the foul
" of a fellow that never himfelf be-
" lieved he had one to fave. Do
" this, I fay, or I'll befpeak the
" darkeft cell in Bedlam for you,
" and carry you thither myfelf in my
" great-coat pocket, although I muft
" be obliged to give the keeper a
" certificate that you have for fome
" years paffed for a man, elfe he
" will fwear I have brought him an
" Italian greyhound. Then with a
" ftamp, that made him bounce off
" the floor like a pea from the end
" of a boy's piece of broken tobacco-

D 3   " pipe,

" pipe, I turned about and left him.
" What effect my advice had on him
" I can't tell, but my coat did not
" come home this morning." " No,"
fays the gentleman to whom he was
telling his tale, " nor can it come
" home till night; for I faw the lan-
" thorn-jaw'd rogue coming out of the
" Tabernacle amongft the thick of
" them, turning up the white of his
" eyes with more devotion than even
" mother Cole herfelf. So that all
" thefe amazing cool arguments of
" yours had no more effect on the
" infatuated varlet——than a city
" Remonftrance has on a determin'd
" ——and your next fuit and mine,
" (for I likewife employ the mifera-
" ble object,) muft have feven and
" twenty-penny worth of extraordi-
" nary cabbage pared off the fkirts,
" to

" to make up the difference betwixt
" three shillings and a five and three-
" penny piece."

CHAP. V.

A new fashioned handkerchief for a
courtier.

HERE my owner was called upon by Long Sir Timothy to go
to the play; so up he started, and
bid the waiter take pay for his dish
of coffee, and bring change; but
Sir Timothy stopped the fellow, and
after wiping his nose with the inside
of his coat lap, told him to save the
trouble of bringing change for the
six-pence, he would drink a dish of
coffee himself. On which, having

two

minutes to fpare, down they both
fat. Sir Timothy then bid the waiter
bring a large flice of bread and butter, which, being inftantly done, he
rammed it down with as much cele-
rity as the Norfolk farmers bolt
their flices of bacon; then fwal-
lowing the coffee fo hot that it would
have fcalded Powell the fire-eater,
he ftarted up, and fhot like lightning, out of the room, for fear the
waiter fhould overtake him, and afk
for pay for his bread and butter:
my owner not being able to get fo
quick after him, becaufe his fword
was a little entangled as he rofe from
his feat, I heard the waiter fay,
" Score Sir Timothy a piece of bread
and butter." " Not I," fays the woman at the bar, " I gave over fcor-
" ing when it came to a hundred,
" and

"and that's a year since." When my owner came out he found Sir Timothy waiting for him very contentedly in the rain; for altho' he had been at court that day, yet he was very sensible the rain could do very little damage to his uncurl'd tie wig, and rusty thread-bare black coat, darned under both sleeves, and the lining pieced on the corner of that skirt he so frequently made use of for a handkerchief; he therefore stood contentedly with his hat under his arm, bidding defiance to wind and weather; but neither my owner's hair or cloaths being weather-proof he called lustily for a coach; as we were nigh a stand we heard a chirrup to the horses, and the crack of a whip at the same instant. Whilst the ragged Jehu was

drawing

drawing up to the foot pavement, a man had got hold of Sir Timothy, and was preffing him in a very miferable tone to pay his fmall bill; for, by the help of feveral as good cuftomers as himfelf, he and his family were ftarving. "Sir Timothy," fays Mr. Villiers—" " pay that poor " " creature, he feems to want it." " Rot him," fays the knight of the greafy fkirt, " he always attacks me " when I have no change in my pock- " et; I have not a note lefs than fifty, " and he only wants five guineas; " can you lend me as much?" "Yes," fays Mr. Villiers, and inftantly put the money into his hand. On which Sir Timothy called the fellow afide, told him to be at the coffee houfe immediately after the play, and have his receipt ready figned; then whipp'd into the

coach

coach after Mr. Villiers, drew up
the glafs, and left the man to wait
with his receipt, either in the rain or
the coffee-houfe, which he pleafed;
where the poor devil may be waiting till now for Sir Timothy—who,
I'll take upon me to fay, won't· fee
the infide of that coffee-houfe again
thefe twelve months, for fear the
poor creature and his receipt fhould
be waiting ftill. Thus, reader, what
to you and me would have been a
ftrange embarraffment, proved to
the long-legged knight a lucky excufe to borrow, or to fpeak more
properly, to fteal five guineas; for
we call it borrowing where there is
an intent to pay, but no man can
accufe the worthy knight of ever fuffering fuch a thought to enter either
into his head or heart. Why I call

it

it a lucky excuse is, because the knight had long before so quite exhausted the whole catalogue of excuses, such as changing his breeches in a hurry; forgetting to call at his banker's; lending a worthy good-natured fellow as he came along all the money in his pocket, *cum multis aliis*, that he began in his old age to be a little at a loss for fresh excuses, the stale ones being as well known to all his acquaintance as his long legs and lank tye-wig; therefore Mr. Villiers furnished him with a lucky excuse, by desiring him to pay the poor man; and for his reward, I'll take upon me to assure him, that himself and the poor receipt-writer will neither of them have reason to boast of being first paid.

After

After the play was finished, Mr.
Villiers looked for his friend Sir Timothy; but he, worthy foul, not
expecting another five-guinea excuse could possibly happen that
night, had given him the slip.
As Mr. Villiers was but a new
acquaintance of Sir Timothy's, having accidentally eaten a mutton-
chop together that day, and there
made an appointment to go to the
play, he dreamed of little less than
finishing the evening over a bottle
with his new long-shank'd friend,
and therefore hastened back to the
coffee-house, where he, as well as
myself, heard Sir Timothy order the
receipt-bearer to attend. No Sir
Tim—could he see there; but he
took notice of an industrious looking man that sat in a corner, watching

ing, the door, who he naturally
gueſſed was the gentleman in waiting; but was further convinced it
muſt be the ſame, becauſe whenever
the door opened, the man looked
up rather higher than the top of it,
whereas for a middle ſized man people caſt their eyes not much higher
than the centre of the entrance; however, the poor man kept ſipping his
three-penny worth of punch by tea-
ſpoonfuls to make it laſt, and Mr.
Villiers kept reading the news-papers
over and over again, till the hour
began to approach,

When midnight wolves howl through the
dreary waſte;

but no Sir Timothy came. The expecting parties might have ſtaid till
doomſday before the expected heroe
would

would ever have thought of them; his long legs had carried his long body in search of another five-guinea touch;—whether he found one or not, if ever I have the good luck to hear, you shall certainly know.

CHAP. VI.

A sleepy subject.

THE poor man having given over all hopes of seeing the knight of the woeful countenance, —with a heavy sigh swallowed the last tea spoonful of his punch; then putting his hand to his pocket, with an air better imagin'd than describ'd, making a face as if he was going to draw his bowels out instead of his

money,

money, he advanced to the bar to difcharge his great reckoning. Mr. Villiers, who only read with one eye, and, like the departed doctor, look'd fharp about him with the other, had too much fenfibility to let fuch a thing efcape him : he afked the man as he paffed by him, " if he had not " been waiting for Sir Timothy ?" he anfwered with as long an afpiration, as if he was fucking the word up from the fole of ·his foot, " Yes, Sir;" " Then," fays Mr. Villiers, "as I was " partly the occafion of your lofing " fo much time, you muft give me " leave to pay the little expence you " have been at," and inftantly or-dered the waiter to bring fix-penny worth of punch more for the good man—he thank'd him with an air of gratitude, and replied, " Yes, Sir, " the

" the lofs of my time was hard upon
" me to-night, for I was going where
" I fhould have earned half a
" crown to have bought my fa-
" mily a dinner to-morrow, inftead
" of which, after I had paid for
" my glafs of punch, I fhould
" have gone home with one fingle
" halfpenny in my pocket." " What
" trade are you?" fays Mr. Villiers;
" I was," fays the man, " a cabinet-
" maker in good repute, but the cuf-
" tom of two great men entirely
" broke me; and, at prefent, I fup-
" port my family by doing little
" jobbs, and picking up a picture,
" or fitting up a curious little cabi-
" net now and then; and this debt
" of Sir Timothy's is for a picture
" that he fold at an auction for five
" and twenty guineas, only by add-
" ing a three-guinea frame to it,

" which was never paid for." " Have
" you ever a cabinet by you at pre-
" fent ?" fays Mr. Villiers ;—" Yes,
" Sir," fays the man, " I have the
" prettieft little thing you ever faw,
" and have fitted it up fo well,
" that it is not only as good
" to appearance, but alfo better in
" reality than a new one. I can
" afford it for two guineas, tho'
" it was never made for twelve."
" Then," fays Mr. Villiers, " pray
" bring it to the third houfe in———
" Street, in the morning; here is a
" guinea by way of earneft; and if
" it anfwers your defcription, which
" I don't doubt, I fhall give you
" three guineas inftead of two for
" it." The livelieft fancy can hardly
form an idea of the furprifing change
this made in the man's countenance ;

he

I

he took the guinea, but was unable
to utter more than, " Thank you,
" Sir, Sir, I thank you ; thank you,
" Sir, Sir, I thank you." Thefe words
I believe he would have repeated
as often as there are changes on fix
bells, if the waiter had not brought
him the glafs of punch, which chang'd
his tone into " Your health, Sir,—
" Sir, your good health." Then
drinking it off with more fatisfaction
than the man that got the laft pa-
tent of a thoufand a year could do
for the foul of him, he made a bow,
wherein gratitude was as ftrongly
painted as ingratitude is in the face
of * * * *

In the morning the poor man,
for fear of miffing the hour of ten,
the time appointed, was there at

half

half paſt ſeven. Mr. Villiers, who
generally roſe at eight, hearing he
was below, ſent for him and his cabinet up: it really anſwered the
man's deſcription, but had coſt twice
the ſum he ſaid, at leaſt; he
had taken ſurpriſing pains in fitting
it up, and Mr. Villiers, who was a
judge, *ſoon ſaw its value*, he therefore gave him five guineas beſides
his earneſt; the man took up only
two, and ſaid, " that was enough of
" all conſcience, and he thank'd him
" kindly: but Mr. Villiers told him,
" although it might be enough for
" ſuch a reaſonable man to aſk, yet
" *it was not enough for him to give.*"
This ended all diſputes, and the ca-
binet-maker went home as happy as
a prince, leaving Mr. Villiers not
only delighted with the opportunity
of

serving an honeſt induſtrious man, but actually ten or eleven pounds richer than he was the minute before the five guineas walked out of his purſe into Sir Timothy's breeches-pocket; where, notwithſtanding the ſhifts and ſhirks he practiſes daily to obtain a few guineas, he always puts them ſo hot into that long pocket, that they burn the bottom out.

C H A P. VII.

Pop in, and pop out.

MR. Villiers, though a man of faſhion, and kept the beſt company, yet delighted in variety; for which reaſon he ſeldom miſs'd

being

being once or twice a fortnight at an
agreeable club of merchants, and
better kind of tradefmen, who met
three days in the week at the Crown
and Anchor, where he took a fancy
to a little hatter, becaufe he perceived
him, at the bottom, an honeft, well-
meaning man; he therefore not only
bought all his own hats of him, but
got him good cuftom by recommen-
dations. Now this honeft little fellow being a bachelor, keeps but
one fervant, which he calls a maid
of all work. When he gets drunk,
which doth not happen above feven times a week, he is never fo
happy as when he is expatiating on
the virtues of this virgin of his,
efpecially her fobriety. One evening, when Mr. Villiers carried me to
the club, whether this honeft man
had

had drank more than ordinary, or the vehemence with which he recounted the praifes of this maid of all work, had driven the fumes of his liquor with more velocity than ufual into his pericranium, I know not, but fo it happened, that the brufher of new and old hats almoft entirely loft the ufe of his legs. My owner would have put him into a coach, but there was no fnch thing as perfuading him, nothing being fo certain, as that the more any man is overtaken, the foberer he fancies himfelf; therefore walk home he would, in fpite of all Mr. Villiers could fay; the confequence was, the firft ftep he made after he quitted the iron rails, as he went down the ftreet-door fteps—carried him in a fine circumvendibus reel quite a-

crofs

crofs the ftreet, where, luckily for
him, but unluckily for herfelf, a
poor woman happened to be carrying home a bundle of dirty linen
to wafh; againft her hips did his
head come with fuch a thump,
that it fent her headlong on the
foot path, with the bundle rolling
four or five yards before her; the
woman thinking fhe was knocked
down with a blow on the head, inftead of the tail, roared out, fire!
thieves! and murder! fo nimbly, that
although fhe pronounced every fyl-
lable diftinctly, yet to me they appeared but one fhort word. Mr.
Villiers, who never fufpected the
little dyer of hats would make fuch
a quick excurfion, and was therefore looking if he had not fallen
threugh the iron-bars into the area,

foon

soon guessed by the shrilness of the tone what was the matter; he therefore whipped a-cross the street to set affairs to rights before the watchmen's lanthorns, which he saw hobbling along from different avenues, should approach too nigh; being sensible that these gentlemen, like true peace-officers, always help to bring a skirmish to a serious battle, and then avail themselves of the consequence; a shilling, and some assistance to find her bundle, had sent the poor woman off, with a curtsey, before the hobbling lanthorn-bearers arrived. Now the whole group of midnight magistrates, within the attraction of the voice, consisted of three (who, altho' not good men and true, were the best the parish could pick up) they agreed nem. con.

that

that it was a female voice; therefore taking the little hatter for a woman difguifed in men's cloaths, afk'd her if any body was going to ravifh her.

I have heard fome knowing people fay, the firft time a man is on fhipboard, he fancies that every thing he fees on fhore, whether hedges, trees, or churches, or houfes, all move, becaufe he is not fenfible of the motion of the machine he is in. Thus it fared with our little drunken hatter, he ftill thought himfelf as fober as a judge, and therefore fancied both the watchmen and their lanthorns drunk, becaufe to him they appeared to reel about; he therefore hickup'd out in a very rough voice, he thought them mighty fad

fellows

z

fellows for getting fo drunk on their ftations, that they did not know a man from a woman. My owner forefeeing a difagreeable altercation was likely to arife between the drunken fool and fober knaves, told the ftouteft of them he would give him fix-pence to help him to fee the gentleman home : a bargain was immediately ftruck, and away we went, and foon reached the door of the hat-maker's houfe. The firft thing my owner did was to difmifs the watchman ; then knocking at the door, waited to deliver his overtaken friend into the hands of this peerlefs maid of all work, not doubting but fhe knew how to get her mafter to bed, let him be ever fo far gone.

After

After exercifing the rapper three
or four times, and waiting a good
fpace between each rap, the door
at laft opened, and we perceived a
figure ftanding upright againft the
wainfcot, which happened to be
this jewel of a maid of all work,
who being a very good girl, had
fympathized with her good mafter
fo much, that fhe had kept drinking
bumper for bumper with him the
whole night. My owner told her,
her mafter was a little overtaken,
fo he was refolved to deliver him into her care; "Yes," fays fhe, with
a hickup that would not have dif-
graced a Dutchman, and ftretching
out her hand to take him, came
tumbling out of the door the inftant
the hat-maker was tumbling in. In
this dilemma what could my owner

do?

do ? To leave the diftreffed damfel all her length in the ftreet, would have been cruel; and to help the fervant before the mafter, was falfe heraldry; however, the bias that every honeft man poffeffes towards the fofter fex, prevailed on him to give the preference to Peggy; fo to work he fell with her, and got her up to the threfhold, where he found the hatter had fome how or other raifed his own body, and was tumbling over the threfhold out again. My owner fearing he would hurt himfelf, made a catch at him, by which means he let Peggy tumble in, and could not prevent Johnny from tumbling out. Zooks, thinks I, this is furely a Dutch weather-houfe, when the man goes in, the woman comes out, and when the woman goes in, the

the man comes out; they seem indeed to do it in a sort of a hurry, but that may be owing to the sudden change of the weather; this was only my first thought, but on second thoughts (like most Englishmen) I found I was wrong.

Now that Peggy was laid safe in the passage, Johnny in the street was the object of my owner's attention; but first he thought proper, as the watchman's box was not forty yards from the place, to crave his worship's assistance; after begging pardon for disturbing his rest, and talking of six-pence, the found of which penetrated through his worship's thrum cap, the bearer of the staff and lanthorn started up directly, and in an instant disengaged one ear from

from its woollen coverlid, to listen
further about this six-penny jobb. To
those that wallow in riches, such as
contractors, commissaries, gover-
nors, nabobs, parliament-menwith
pensions, and pimps that are paid on
both sides, the sound of six-pence
may not appear so considerable an
object, as it did to our sleep-catch-
ing watchman; but to five millions
of his majesty's subjects, especially
towards the North, a silver six-pence
is a valuable piece of coin: you must
not wonder then, if this trusty officer
of the night, at the agreeable sound,
not only shook the god Morpheus
from off his shoulders in an instant,
but assumed as much alertness as if
he had neither seen or heard of him
that evening.

By

By the help of this tremendous
knight of the burning lanthorn, my
owner got Johnny raised off the
pavement, and safely conducted into
his own dining-room. Peggy having
kept a good fire in it for two reasons,
viz. first to drink, and next to sleep
by, made the room feel pure and
comfortable; here they laid Johnny
down on the carpet, a standing pos-
ture not agreeing with his constitu-
tion at that period; next they fetch'd
poor Peggy, who, by good luck,
had discovered no inclination for another trip into the street, but lay as
snug in the passage as a printer's devil between two worm-eaten blank-
ets; poor overtaken Peggy they laid
down close by her overtaken master,
without any fear of their overtaking
one another; then my owner, by the

help

help of the farthing candle borrowed from the refulgent lanthorn, found his way up to Johnny's bed, or Peggy's bed, call it which you please, for if you will allow two pillows to be creditable witnesses, the bed belonged to them both; but be that as it may, my owner brought both the pillows down, along with the quilt and a blanket, which he carefully spread over them, and put a pillow under each of their heads, then letting down the latch of the street-door, and half-locking it on the outside, he put the key in his pocket, and marched very soberly home.

CHAP.

CHAP. VIII.

A more serious adventure.

I Ended my last chapter with saying we marched very soberly
home, I should have said, homeward; but many accidents, all sai-
lors know, happen in a homeward
bound voyage: this was our case;
we did not reach home by some
hours so soon as was expected; for
passing through Bartholomew-Lane,
at the back gate of the Bank, we
heard a rough voice say, "Damn
"you, what are you? Or how
"the devil came you to stand shi-
"vering and starving here?" A
foft

soft female voice replied to this elegant speech, " Pray, Sir, leave me; " I don't disturb you, why should " you disturb me ?" this excited my owner's curiosity, who began to move towards the place just as the first eloquent orator had opened his lips again. He therefore halted a moment, that he might not quite interrupt him, " Damn you, for a " bitch," says the orator, " what! you " pretend to modesty, do you ? go " with me and be damn'd, and " drink a pint of hot purl." " I " pretend to nothing, Sir, says she, " but to die in peace, if mankind " will let me." These words, and the tone with which they were uttered, had an instantaneous effect on my owner's sensibility, he therefore hastened up to the place, and said to the man,

whom

whom he found to be a drunken journeyman-fhoemaker, "Why do "you ufe this poor creature thus, "friend?" "What's that to you, "and be d——d;" fays Crifpin, "fhe is my prize, and if you don't "go about your bufinefs, I'll make "you, you jamfootering fon of "a French whore." My owner, whofe feelings were delicate to the higheft degree, made it a rule never to fay a rude thing, or ever take one; therefore, not being mafter of that fort of oratory in which the fhoemaker dealt, he return'd his compliment with his fift, and at one ftroke fent Crifpin's head to perform the part of the paviour's ftamper by ramming down the ftones, which it did in fo complete a manner, you might have heard the found as far as that heavy lump of build-

ing

ing called the Manfion-houfe. Crifpin, who did not like the blow on
his right cheek fo well as to offer his
left, wifely lay ftill to take time to
digeft what he had got, being pretty
well convinced a fecond dofe would
not much mend the matter. In the
interim my owner advancing to the
corner of the gate, where the poor
young creature ftood as much in
the fhade as poffible, was furprized
to fee a very well-dreffed lady all in
tears, and ready to fink into the
earth, he afked her, in his engaging
manner, " if he could be of any fer-
" vice to her?" " O, Sir," fays fhe,
with a voice fweeter than the notes
of the tuneful nightingale, " can
" you fhew me a place where I may
" quietly lay down my wearied limbs
" and die?" " Madam," fays my

owner,

owner, (beyond meafure touch'd with the fweetnefs of her voice, and the manner of expreffing herfelf,) "I can with more pleafure "fhew you a place that will contri- "bute to preferve a life fo much "worth taking care of, as yours "feems to be." "I believe, Sir," fays the lady, "all that care will be "fruitlefs; I feel my heart is already "broken, and, I thank heaven, I "am haftening faft to my diffolution, "without the enormous fin of fui- "cide, which I have all this day been "tempted to commit; twice was I "at the river-fide, and as often did "my guardian-angel warn me back, "and now a fettled refignation to the "will of Heaven has taken poffeffion "of my foul, and I am all obedi- "ence to its juft decrees; it was its "will,

" will, that by the hands of cruel,
" deceitful man, I should be stripp'd
" of every thing that could render
" life supportable, except my honour
" and innocence, which the inhu-
" man wretch could not strip me of;
" to me they are an unspeakable com-
" forts; but of what use are they
" in procuring friends, or even the
" mere necessaries of life?" My
owner, struck to the heart with her
stile and sweet delivery, was devour-
ing her words, when he perceived
her fainting away, he catched her in
his arms, and bearing her to the
steps, sat himself down and support-
ed her; she continued insensible for
a quarter of an hour at least, during which time an empty chair
came accidentally by. When the
poor distressed lady was enough

recovered to be able to support herself on the seat, he put her into the chair, assuring her, she should be carried to a place of honour and safety; the scoundrel shoemaker had silently decamped when he found my owner so busy in supporting the poor lady, for fear of getting a little more of what he was conscious he deserved. Mr. Villiers ordered the chairman to go very slow, and would not quit the side a moment, till they came to St. Paul's Church-Yard, where luckily finding a coach, with great difficulty he lifted her in, she being already grown so weak, that she was scarce able to stand, much less to mount up a step without help ; he seated himself by her, and, during the time of driving to the west-end of the town, he gave her the strongest

assu-

affurances of carrying her to a place of fafety. She politely told him, " fhe could fufpect nothing wrong " from a gentleman of his nice feel- " ings and fenfibility, which fhe " plainly perceived during the time " of her fhort converfation with him;" but could not help adding in broken accents, " why did it not " pleafe heaven to fend you to my " aid before it was too late?" " It " is not, it fhall not be too late," re- plies he——with uncommon emo- tion, " chear up your fpirits, you " have loft nothing, by your own ac- " count, but what with eafe may be " either recovered or repaired, and " my fortune fhall be devoted to " do both."

This unexpected goodnefs was too much for her fhaken delicate frame, and

and grateful, though broken heart, to bear, and she once more became lifeless, and would have fallen off the seat, if he now had not again caught her in his arms. She was just recovered when they arrived at the hotel in——Street, where he put her into the care of the mistress of the house, a woman of character and reputation, who presently prepared her some cordial, of which the poor creature could taste very little, though, as it afterwards appeared, she was fasting, and had wandered up and down, and about the town, above nine hours in a kind of delirium, having parted, with true spirit and disdain, from the friend at whose house she designed to have taken refuge the night before; this terrible day succeeding a sleepless

night,

4

night, makes it not furprizing that in fo fhort a fpace of time fuch amazing havock was made in fo delicate a frame as hers, for fhe was really a fine form'd creature; her features were amazingly well turned and regular, and there was fomething fo amiably foft, tender, and expreffive in her countenance, as at once indicated her good fenfe and delicate fine feelings, and the goodnefs of her heart was impreffed on every feature, word, and action; thefe qualifications, all aided by a polite education, rendered her a moft truly amiable creature.

CHAP.

C H A P. IX.

The subject of the last chapter continued.

MR. Villiers did not stay long, it being neceſſary for the poor lady to get a little reſt, if the perturbations of her mind would permit it. At parting he left his purſe with the miſtreſs of the houſe, and begg'd, ſhe would take the ſame care of her gueſt, as if ſhe were her own daughter; which ſhe promiſed to do, and was as good as her word; for he found the next day every thing done with the utmoſt tenderneſs and regard: one of the maid ſervants had

attended

attended her bed-fide, and in the morning a careful nurfe was provided; a good old apothecary had been confulted about what was proper to recover her depreffed fpirits; in fhort, Mr. Villiers was pleafed with every thing that had been done; but became diftrefs'd, to the laft degree, when he found that although fhe endeavoured in his prefence to affume a chearful ferenity, yet even her bodily ftrength was greatly impaired in one night; and it was with great difficulty, the nurfe faid, they could lead her from the bed to her chair, where fhe fat fmiling at her approaching diffolution.

Mr. Villiers, whofe heart the night before had fympathized very deeply in her diftrefs, (much more indeed

than

than he even was himself aware of)
feeing the lovely creature, whofe
real charms were fet off to more advantage by her drefs being better ad-
jufted, fitting, if I may ufe an old
expreffion, like Patience on a mo-
nument, could not bear it, but loft
all the philofophy he ufed to value
himfelf upon ; the big round drops
trickled down his manly face, and
all his foul diffolved in tendernefs.
He kneeled and begged fhe would
try to recover her fpirits, if not for
her own, yet for the fake of a man
whofe fate had become involved with
hers. " Nothing," fays the tender
creature, " could add to my diftrefs
" fo much as that thought. I hope
" heaven did not prolong my life a
" day or two to make me the in-
" ftrument of bringing affliction to
" the

" the worthiest of mankind. Let
" not, O gracious God!" adds this
good creature, with eyes lifted up
to heaven, " Oh, let not the short
" space of time thou hast been
" pleased further to prolong my life,
" be the innocent means of giving
" pain to any created being, much
" less to the man thou hast endowed
" with so benevolent a heart." These
words, the sweet manner of express-
ing them, and the goodness of heart,
which at that time shone clearer
than the sun in its meridian, from
every feature in her face, had quite
the contrary effect to what the lovely
creature designed it. From that
moment his soul took fellowship
with hers; and he formed a resolu-
tion either to recover her, or not
survive her: perhaps such a resolu-
tion

tion may be thought sudden; but
you will cease to wonder at it, if you
consider, that when all the faculties
are beforehand melted into such tenderness, every fresh impression must
strike amazingly deep. Just then Doctor * * * whom Mr. Villiers had before sent for, came in ; after feeling
her pulse, and asking a few ques-
tions, seeing the concern visible on
Mr. Villiers's face, he took him into
another room to enquire the origin
and cause of the lady's disorder.
From Mr. Villiers's account the
good man was confirmed in the
thoughts his skill at the first view
had suggested of the lady's dangerous situation ; but seeing grief painted in such strong colours in Mr.
Villiers's face, he forbore to speak
his thoughts, hoping, nay, ardently
wishing

wishing his skill might this time be deceived. How unlike is this good man to some wretches of the faculty, who, rather than their skill should be called in question, would sooner help a patient into his coffin, than set him upon his legs, supposing their ignorance really knew how.

The good Doctor told Mr. Villiers, that after two or three visits he should be able to form some judgment; at the same time assuring him, that being still and quiet was the only probable method of restoring her, and therefore it would be absolutely necessary for him to leave her alone. They then both returned into her room, where, whilst the good man was prescribing something to raise the poor lady's spirits a little, Mr. Villiers, with an endearing tenderneſs, too expreſſive to be deſcrib'd in words, was begging her to forget her ſorrows, and live for both their ſakes; then retired with the worthy Doctor, but ſeem'd to leave his ſoul and all the faculties of life behind.

About two o'clock the next day, Mr. Villiers went back to the place where he had left his ſoul; he found the amiable creature with pen and ink before her. " I have, Mr. Vil- " liers," ſays ſhe, at his entrance, " been writing above an hour." " Why would my dear angel," ſays, he, " fatigue herſelf at this critical, " very critical time?" " Becauſe," re- plies the tender-hearted maid, " it " was neceſſary you ſhould know " who.

" who I am ; and to tell it to a man
" of your fenfibility, would have dif-
" trefs'd me fo much, that I fhould
" never have got through it. But
" now that my fpirits are a little fub-
" fided, I recollect that there is left
" in the hands of that undeferving
" woman, where I lodged, too ma-
" ny effects for thirty pounds, efpe-
" cially as there are jewels, that were
" my mother's, of the real value of
" more than five hundred pounds ;
" but my diftraction did not fuffer
" me to think of them." Then deli-
vering an inventory of all her cloaths,
&c. the particulars of which fhe
had recollected as well as fhe could,
" and that," fays fhe, (giving him
another paper) " is a fhort account
" of the unhappy creature that your
" compaffion would have faved,

" had

" had it pleafed Heaven I had
" known you a day fooner; but
" the pleaiure it gives me to have
" met with fuch a worthy man, is
" greatly allayed by the anxiety I
" have unwillingly grafted in your
" generous bofom. Take my ef-
" fects," adds fhe, " out of the hands
" of that worldly-minded creature;
" I fhall feel a pleafure in leaving
" them in the hands of a man that
" will make fo charitable a ufe of
" them as you will." " Talk not
" of ufe for them," fays Mr. Villiers,
with a mixture of the greateft tendernefs and anguifh, " but live, not
" only to make ufe yourfelf of
" them, but of every thing my for-
" tune can procure you " " Ah!
" call not my foul back," fays the
lovely fufferer, " from the path of
" refig-

" refignation, where it is travelling
" to deliver itfelf up into the hands
" of the Divine Creator; nor make
" me quit, with regret, a world
" that I had with pleafure refign'd
" all defires to dwell in. I would
" deny nothing that your generous
" heart would afk, but this requeft
" is out of my power; the fatal
" blow is ftruck, and Heaven's will
" be done."

Never was fuch a ftriking picture
of forrow and defpair exhibited, as
appeared at this inftant in the face
of Mr. Villiers. I thought he would
have funk directly into the earth;
he remained fpeechlefs for a confi-
derable time, whilft ftrong convul-
fions feemed to fhake his whole
frame. At laft, the woman's, part

of

of his compofition came to his aid,
and tears gave relief to thofe con-
vulfive emotions, which elfe muft
certainly have been fatal; tears
courfed each other down his manly
cheeks, and form'd a rapid current
o'er his garments. At that inftant
the worthy Doctor * * * came in: he
had feen the poor diftreffed lady a-
bout two hours before, and had
formed a refolution of telling Mr.
Villiers his thoughts about the danger he apprehended fhe was in; but
feeing him fo much more interefted
in her welfare than he could have
furmifed, he was puzzled what to
fay; altho' this third, gave him ftill
lefs hopes than the firft and fecond
vifit. He faw her diforder, which he
at firft clearly perceived arofe from
fome fatal calamity, made dreadful
havock

havock of her tender frame, and that she was hastening to that long home, from whence none ever yet returned : he therefore advised Mr. Villiers not only to suppress those emotions, but to absent himself for an hour, as his presence much accelerated an event he so much dreaded. Mr. Villiers took his advice, and, with the most endearing accent, begged of her to try to live, and follow that worthy man's directions. Then retiring into the next room, took out the papers to read the account of the unfortunate possessor of his heart; the contents of which were as follows: but if I don't transmit them to my reader in as delicate and expressive terms as that pretty young creature did, it is no fault of mine; for her stile was,

like

like her manners and actions, in-
mitable.

C H A P. X.

*Continuation of the story of Miss St.
Vincent.*

" **I** Am," says this delicate, wor-
" thy, unhappy young lady,
" the daughter of a West-India
" gentleman, whose father left
" him a very rich plantation; but
" coming into possession of it at
" the age of twenty-two, five
" years thoughtless round of plea-
" sures in and about town, join'd
" with the robberies, as I may call
" them, that all agents abroad will
" be guilty of when they find their
" masters

" masters running behind hand, had
" so greatly impaired my father's ef-
" fects, that he found it highly ne-
" cessary to go over himself to take
" care of what little was left, car-
" rying with him my mother, the
" daughter of a deceased baronet,
" who he had married not eighteen
" months before, and whose fortune
" of five thousand pounds had only
" served to stop the current of duns
" for a very short space. I had then
" seen the light about three months,
" and was left under the care of the
" worthy Mr. Bonheart, my father's
" factor in town His, and his wife's
" care of my education I should ever
" have remembered with gratitude,
" had Heaven prolonged my life
" beyond the common space allotted
" to the race of man, although the
" un-

" unworthy fon of that worthy pair,
" has thus cut me off in the flower of
" my age. My father, notwithftand-
" ing he had a very fine eftate left,
" yet contriving, as four-fifths of the
" planters do, to be always a year
" behind hand, and of confequence
" being forced to fell cheaper and
" buy dearer than his provident
" neighbours, went rather back every
" year; fo that at his death, which
" happened when I was about fe-
" venteen, the fmall matter he left
" me was in a moft perplexed con-
" dition.   My mother had been re-
" leafed from the calamities of this
" frail life about a year before my
" father, fo that he luckily appointed
" the worthy Mr. Bonheart his fole
" executor, in truft for me, with
" power to fell, and do every
                              " thing

" thing he thought proper for my
" advantage, without being liable
" to be called to account even
" by myfelf. The extent of the
" truft pleafed the good man, and
" he repaid his confidence by care
" and tendernefs for his daughter.
" The perplex'd remains of my fa-
" ther's fortune, which he was told,
" when all the debts were paid,
" would not be clear five hundred
" pounds, did this good man, by his
" affiduity, and thorough knowledge
" of the world, fo well difpofe of,
" that when I came to the age of
" twenty-one, he delivered over to
" me Bank-ftock for near ten thou-
" fand pounds, refufing at the fame
" time the ufual commiffion, for
" what he had been at the trouble
" to manage in fo advantageous a
                        " manner :

" manner : nor did he leave a fin-
" gle debt of my father's unpaid.
" Whether he felt himfelf in a de-
" clining ftate of health, which made
" him fo defirous to fettle with me,
" I can't fay, but he did not furvive
" this act of uncommon friendfhip
" above a month, leaving his for-
" tune, which was reputed to be a-
" bout fifteen or twenty thoufand
" pounds, to his only fon, who,
" though a wild young man, always
" regardlefs of bufinefs to all ap-
" pearance, feemed to have fome
" good qualities in him : but, alas !
" that appearance, I find, was only
" to me, who wifhed to think well
" of the fon of fuch kind benefac-
" tors as both the father and mo-
" ther had been to me. Unhappily
" his mother had been dead two

" years

" years before his father, elſe had
" I been with her ; and ſhe, knowing
" him much better than me, would
" have ſaved me out of the ſnare in-
" to which my inexperience let me
" fall.

" Upon the marriage of a widow
" lady, a relation of my guardian's,
" with whom he plac'd me in the
" country when his wife died, be-
" ing then left to myſelf, I came
" to town, and took a ready-fur-
" niſh'd lodging at ſixty pounds a
" year in —— Street. About a fort-
" night after I was ſettled, young
" Mr. Bonheart came to pay me a
" viſit. I received him as a ſiſter
" would a brother, and indeed uſu-
" ally call'd him ſo, looking upon
" him as my foſter brother, for his
                                    " father

" father and mother had been the
" tenderest of parents to me. He
" assum'd the air of a man of bu-
" siness ; told me that now the care
" of his own affairs were fallen up-
" on him, he felt more pleasure in
" regulating his own concerns, than
" he ever did in all the hours of his
" wild extravagance; that business
" went on swimmingly, and that if
" the old gentleman had left him
" twice as much, he could employ
" it every penny, not only in the
" service of his friends abroad, but
" with great advantage to himself.
" And, Polly," says he, with a care-
" less air peculiar to himself, " when
" I am worth fifty thousand, and
" can support you as you ought to
" be, I'll then make my addresses
" to you." I laugh'd, and told
" him,

6

" him, we were too near a-kin; for I
" always really look'd upon him as
" my brother. After a little more
" converſation we parted. At going
" out, I deſired he would call any
" time that did not interfere with
" buſineſs, which he did two or
" three times in a fortnight, not
" ſtaying above ten minutes, pre-
" tending hurry of buſineſs, and
" ſaying, " It is all long of you,
" Polly; for I will be worth half a
" plumb before I ſpeak a word to
" you." I told him, when he was
" worth half a plumb, I would do
" all in my power to help him to a
" good wife; but I never, ſays I,
" can change the ſiſterly affection I
" bear you into any thing elſe.
" I'll try that," ſays he " when I have
" completed my wiſhes, which I
                                    " am

" fo anxous about, that I employ
" every guinea I have in the world,
" and walk the town round many
" a day with two or three shillings
" in my pocket." Here was a bait
" thrown out for an open heart like
" mine, which from the knowledge
" this—(I shudder to call the son
" of my benefactor, villain, yet,
" alas ! I fear the name is too good
" for him ;) I shall therefore say,
" from the knowledge that this bad
" man had of me, could hardly fail
" of success. What need you,
" (says I) run yourself so close, when
" you know I can always assist you
" for a little time with five hundred,
" or even a thousand pounds, upon
" an emergency : if I was to lose a
" thousand in helping the son of my
" benefactor it would do me no great
                                    " damage,

7

" damage, becaufe it would be only
" a gown a year lefs. " Polly, " fays
" this hypocrite, " I would not fuffer
" you, who have nothing but your in-
" tereft to live upon, to rifque a thou-
" fand pounds; trade is precarious,
" even with the moft careful, though
" I take the greateft precautions
" imaginable; but as far as five hun-
" dred goes, when I can make a con-
" fiderable advantage of it, I'll trou-
" ble you to truft me a fortnight or
" three weeks with that fum; an op-
" portunity may happen, perhaps in
" two or three days, perhaps not in
" a month." Saying this we parted.

" To make fhort a ftory which
" draws the vital blood from
" my heart much fwifter than the
" ink can flow from my pen, he
" got me foon after to fell five hun-

Vol. III.   H   " dred

" dred ſtock for him, and reinſtated
" it punctually in ten days or leſs:
" this he repeated four or five
" times in about ſix months, boaſt-
" ing what great advantage he made
" of it, and apologizing at the ſame
" time for the trouble he gave me
" of going ſo often down to the
" Bank to transfer. I begged of
" him not to think of that, as
" the pleaſure of being uſeful to
" my brother, the ſon of my bene-
" factor, more than repaid twenty
" times the trouble. Thus did this
" vileſt of men carry on the farce
" till two or three days before the
" fatal night you found me ſo for-
" lorn and diſtracted. In the morn-
" ing he came to breakfaſt with me,
" and told me he had been ponder-
" ing all night about me, as my in-

" tereſt

" tereſt was as dear to him as his own.
" Polly," ſays he, " we are at the eve
" of a war; ſtocks began to drop
" yeſterday, and, in a week's time,
" I am ſure will be ten per cent.
" lower." What would you have
" me do, brother? ſays I, " I would
" have you," ſays he, " ſell out this
" very day, and turn your money
" into India bonds; they are at a
" ſmall premium now. ſo nothing
" can be loſt by them; I'll go with
" you to aſſiſt you in ſelling and buy-
" ing; then, to keep you ſafe from
" all accidents of fire and thieves, I
" will call with you to lodge the bonds
" at Child's, where they will be ſafe.
" I am certain this day's work will
" be a thouſand pounds difference
" to my dear ſiſter." Every thing
" appeared ſo clear to me, eſpecially

H 2   " his

" his care in the laſt article of lodg-
" ing the bonds ſo ſafe, that, after
" a little more diſcourſe, I ordered
" a coach, and drove with him down
" to the city: we got out at his
" hoſier's, in whoſe dining-room I
" ſat till he fetch'd his broker, who
" brought a purchaſer along with
" him; and we croſſed over to the
" Bank, where I transferred ſtock
" to the value of nine thouſand ſe-
" ven hundred pounds. To ſave me
" the trouble, he counted the Bank-
" notes as he took them from the
" broker, deſiring me to overlook
" him to ſee if he received right;
" then wrapping them up, held out
" his hand in the poſture of pre-
" ſenting them to me, but ſuddenly
" turned to the broker, and deſir'd
" him to fetch his friend with the
" India-

" India-bonds directly, and come
" to us at the hofier's: then hold-
" ing the notes in his left hand, and
" puting out his right arm for me
" to lean upon, we walk'd to the
" hofier's; I had juft fet my foot on
" the ftep into the fhop, when he
" pretended to fee the broker with
" the bonds. " Go up ftairs, fifter,"
" fays he, " and I'll overtake him,
" and be with you in a moment."
" He did not, however, return in
" lefs than half an hour, which made
" me think he ftaid long; but at laft
" he came with fo well-meaning a
" face, that I was angry with my-
" felf for being uneafy. " Polly,"
" fays he, " I found that Mr. Sharp
" the broker could not bring fo large
" a fum, without the affurance of a
" banker having money ready to pay

H 3   " for

" for them, fo I lodged the money
" in your name at Meffrs.———and
" got them to give him a line that
" the cafh was ready there; fo they
" will receive the bonds, and have
" them ready for us in the morning.
" But now I think of it, I might
" have lodg'd the notes in my own
" name, becaufe it will give you the
" trouble of coming again into the
" city to-morrow; though, on re-
" collection, as it would be prudent
" to carry them to Child's directly,
" your journey hither is not much
" further than to Temple-Bar. He
" then order'd my fervant to call a
" coach with fo eafy an air, that for
" the life of me I could not fufpect
" any thing wrong, but went home,
" thoroughly fatisfied he would call
" on me at breakfaft in the morning;
" but

" but no Mr. Bonheart came. I was
" fomething alarmed; but about
" two o'clock I received a note that
" Mr. Sharp had only procured five
" thoufand, and could not get the reft
" till the morrow, when he would
" finifh, and I might have them all
" together; this quieted me again:
" but in the morning, when no Mr.
" Bonheart appeared, about twelve
" o'clock I ordered a coach, and
" taking nobody but the footman
" with me, drove inftantly to his
" houfe; I flew directly in, and afk-
" ing for the maid Nanny, an old
" fervant that lived with his father;
" fhe met me with fuch looks of
" horror and difmay upon her coun-
" tenance, as fhock'd me to the laft
" degree. " Oh! madam," fays
" Nanny, " what brought you hi-

H 4   " ther ?"

" ther ?" " I came," fays I, " in
" fearch of your mafter." " I hope,"
" fays the poor creature, " he has
" not been borrowing money of you,
" for all the neighbours fay, he is
" gone off Heaven knows what in
" debt, and has taken in all the friends
" and acquaintance that would truft
" him; I was afraid fomething of
" this fort would happen, for he ne-
" ver minded bufinefs at all, but
" lay fix nights out of feven in fome
" bad houfe in Covent-Garden, or
" fat up all night gaming; we have
" not feen him fince the other day
" morning, and I am afraid is is too
" true, for here has been a hundred
" duns at the door fince he went,
" and they fay, bailiffs will be in
" the houfe to-morrow." At thefe
" words I funk down upon the floor;
" the

" the poor creature did all in her
" power to affift me, and brought
" me to myfelf, when I told her how
" he had ferved me : Barbarous
" wretch, adds I, not to leave me
" a poor thoufand to keep want
" and mifery from the door. The
" old faithful fervant fympathized
" greatly with me in my diftrefs, and
" would fee me home. I fat down
" in my chair in a ftate of infenfi-
" bility, and continued fo till about
" five o'clock, when I was roufed by
" a loud rap at the door of my
" dining-room, which was immedi-
" ately followed by the entrance of
" my landlady, who, in a tone I
" had never been ufed to, addreffed
" me with, " Madam, I have heard
" all your misfortune from the gen-
" tlewoman that fet you home, and
" I am

" I am forry for it; but we that
" have little elfe to depend on but
" the rent of our lodgings, muft look
" to ourfelves; there is half a year's
" rent due to-morrow, and as it is
" not likely you can ftay here, I de-
" fire you will provide yourfelf
" lodgings againft to-morrow night,
" but not a rag of your cloaths fhall
" ftir till I am paid." Had I been
" miftrefs of fpirits enough to
" have anfwered her, aftonifhment
" would have held me mute; but
" fhe gave me no time to reply be-
" fore fhe turned upon her heel and
" went out. Indignation then fup-
" plied the want of fpirits; refolv-
" ing therefore to ftay no longer
" under the roof of a wretch fo loft
" to all fenfe of humanity. I put
" on my cloak, and walked away on
" foot

" foot to the houfe of a woman who
" had been my own maid above
" eleven years, and to whom I had
" given two hundred pounds for
" her portion to an induftrious man
' that kept a kind of grocer's fhop;
" I told her I was come to beg a
" bed of her for a night, or perhaps
" a week or more. She anfwer'd,
" fhe fhould be happy if I would
" make ufe of her fmall apartment
" for a year, or as long as I pleafed;
" then prepared, as fhe faw I was
" faint, to get a difh of tea ready
" as faft as poffible, in the little
" room on the back of the fhop.
" Whilft I was trying to fwallow a
" a fpoonful or two to refrefh me,
" for I was almoft fafting, fhe at-
" tended me with fo much care,
" and feemed to partake fo feelingly
" in

" in the deep affliction she perceived
" I was involved in, that I promised
" to myself some ease, not only in
" disburthening my griefs to her,
" but in receiving the pity and con-
" dolance of such a grateful crea-
" ture; I therefore recounted every
" particular to her, adding what an
" inhuman wretch he was to leave
" me nothing. " Nothing, Madam,"
" says she, with some eagerness:
" no; says I, not so much as will
" pay wages to my man and maid,
" and rent for my lodgings. At
" these words, almost distracted as
" I was, I could perceive the wo-
" man's countenance so chang'd,
" that there was not the least ap-
" pearance of that respectful air it
" always bore in my presence: she
" went abruptly out of the room, on
" pretence

" pretence of serving a customer,
" though her husband was in the
" shop ; then, instead of returning,
" staid consulting with him, serving
" a straggling customer or two as
" they now and then came in, leav-
" ing me alone for about half an
" hour: at last she returned, and
" with an aspect, which was a stran-
" ger to me, having never worn it
" in my presence before, began to
" wash up the china as cooly as if
" I had not been in the room, seem-
" ing all the time big with some-
" thing to which she wanted to give
" utterance : at last it came, " I am
" sorry, Madam," says she, " that
" my husband should be such a
" fool as not to tell me that he this
" very morning let our fore-room to
" a gentleman, and he comes to-
                    " morrow;

" morrow; and gentlemen to be fure
" muft not be difappointed, when
" they have given earneft; but for to-
" night to be fure you are very wel-
" come to our bed." She added a
" great deal more, but the fudden
" fhock of fuch ingratitude had be-
" gun to ftrike too fenfibly on my
" feelings, which drove reafon from
" her throne, and anarchy and con-
" fufion ufurp'd her place. I fix'd
" my eye on the woman fo ftedfaftly,
" without being able to fpeak, that
" fhe could not ftand it, but took
" the china-board, and went to finifh
" her work in the fhop. It was then
" my reafon began to ftagger in ear-
" neft, and I only faintly recollect
" what followed; I remember tak-
" ing my cloak, and walking thro'
" the fhop, where I laid down a fhil-
" ling

" ling on the counter, faying, " that
" is for my tea," with fuch an air of
" difdain, that neither of the fordid
" creatures could anfwer a word; but
" he kept weighing fomething, and
" fhe kept rubbing the tea-pot, as if
" they had never feen me. From that
" moment I can recollect hardly any
" thing, but that I wandered in a
" ftupid kind of infenfibility, and
" muft have walk'd from the hour
" of fix in the evening to three in
" the morning a great number of
" miles; for I gave no reft to the
" fole of my foot, till a few minutes
" before you found me; and had it
" not been for that poor vulgar
" creature, whofe voice brought you
" to the place from whence my fee-
" ble limbs could bear me no fur-
" ther, I fhould long before day-light
　　　　　　　　　　　　" have

" have found eternal reft. I very well
" remember my ejaculation, at Mill-
" bank, where I was going to rufh
" headlong into the Divine Prefence,
" by throwing myfelf into the ftream;
" when the Almighty fuddenly re-
" ftored my reafon, and I faw in its
" proper light the horrid fin of fui-
" cide. Methought I heard my guar-
" dian-angel fay, " Await, Maria,
" with patience, and run with refig-
" nation the race the Almighty hand
" has mark'd out for thee; how
" fhort are the longeft fufferings in
" this world, when compar'd to an
" eternity of happinefs!" ¡On this
" I turn'd with horror from a place
" where I was fo near committing
" fo dreadful a crime, but foon found
" my reafon, by being too bufy in
" making reflections, quickly brought

7   " on

" on a train of ideas, in which she her-
" felf w.s again involved and loft.
" How I reached the New-River I
" know not; but, at Iflington, juft
" as I was again attempting to
" plunge in, it pleafed the Divine
" Goodnefs once more to reftrain
" me. Methought I felt an invi-
" fible hand draw me back; and a
" voice fay, " Rafh girl, tempt not
" the Almighty Creator of heaven
" and earth."

" I then in good earneft refolved
" to bear my afflictions patiently,
" till it fhould pleafe the hand of
" God to lay me down in peace.
" How I wandered to the place
" where you found me I know
" not; I only, as I faid before,
" remember my exhaufted fpirits,

" and wearied limbs would support
" me no further."

C H A P. XI.

*The ſtory of the unhappy injured lady
continued.*

NOthing can equal the different emotions raiſed alternately in the breaſt of Mr. Villiers on reading this account; the villany of young Bonheart did not much ſurprize him, becauſe he knew his character very well; only he could not have ſuppoſed a fiend from hell poſſeſſed of ſo little remorſe, as not to leave a pittance to ſupport life, but entirely deſtroy an amiable young creature, who had as much affection

tion for him as if she had been his real sister : but the vulgar selfishness of the woman of the house, and the ingratitude of her quondam servant, to whom she had been so uncommonly kind, struck him beyond measure ; a flood of love and tenderness for the dear sufferer, mix'd with rage and contempt for the other detestable objects, fix'd him about half an hour on his seat before he could resolve what course to pursue. At last, recollecting that the Doctor had desired him to absent himself as much as he could, to give the poor lady time to recruit her spirits a little, because his presence, and the concern he could not hide, affected her so much ; he therefore thought the properest time offered to go and take care of her

effects ;

effects; fo calling on a gentleman
of the law, defired his affiftance,
and away they went to Mrs. Let-
lodge's houfe. The woman was luckily at home : Mr. Villiers afk'd her,
" if fhe had any lodgings to lett ?"
fhe replied, " fhe had a firft floor ;"
upon which he defired to fee it. The
woman fufpecting nothing of the
matter, and being fenfible that fhewing the lodgings in the neat, elegant
condition the lady had left them,
muft be a great recommendation,
having been embellifhed, by the
pretty creature, with a thoufand neat,
little elegant pieces of furniture of
her own ; the woman therefore conducted them up without hefitation.
Whether a prepoffeffion, in favour of
every thing belonging to the dear
lady was the cafe, I won't fay, but Mr.
Villiers

Villiers was ſtruck beyond meaſure with the neatneſs, taſte, and elegance of the rooms. "Bleſs me!" ſays he, in a kind of ſeeming ſurprize, "by "the toilet and neatneſs, ſome lady "has lodged here?" "Yes;" ſays the woman, compoſedly, "a lady "that went into the country about "a fortnight ago." "Did her ſer- "vants go with her?" ſays Mr. Villiers, gravely: the woman a little diſconcerted at this queſtion, an- ſwered confuſedly, "Yes; no; I "can't tell." "But I can," ſays Mr. Villiers, no longer able to con- tain himſelf, "and our viſit here is "on Miſs St. Vincent's account; this "gentleman has my lord chief juſ- "tice's warrant againſt you, for "locking her ſervants out of her "own lodgings, and ſtealing her

I 3   "goods.

" goods. As no bail can be taken
" in criminal affairs, such as these,
" you must prepare to go with us
" directly." " Dear gentlemen,"
says the woman, ready to sink thro'
the floor, " I have not stirred a rag
" of hers but her jewels, which I
" took into my own room for more
" safety, from whence I will fetch
" them directly." " For more safety,
" deed," says Mr. Villiers; " but
" you must give me leave to attend
" you whilst you fetch them." So
saying, he followed her up to her
own bed-room, where she pulled
the jewels out of a great chest, fill'd
with old gowns and petticoats,
in the centre of which she had
stuffed them. To make short with
this woman, whose company I don't
like at all, they got out of her, that

Miss

Miss St. Vincent's maid-servant had taken the front-garret over the way, where the poor creature sat all day, and most of the night, watching her mistress's return; this devil, the landlady, as Mr. Villiers guessed, having turn'd both her and the foot-man out of doors, the very day after she found Miss Vincent did not return. Upon which Mr. Villiers sent his servant for her, and telling her he had orders to carry her to her mistress, he set both her and the footman to work to pack up all the dear creature's apparel, &c. &c. de-firing the girl to recollect if any thing was wanting, at the same time taking the inventory out of his pocket: on this the woman resolv'd to recollect first, and recollected that she had taken care of the best

I 4   laces,

laces, because they were the most valuable articles after the jewels. I could not help thinking she would have made a fine aid decamp to such a general as * * * * because she could so readily distinguish the cream of the plunder. When all was pack'd up, and put into two coaches, Mr. Villiers still kept up the farce of my lord chief justice's warrant, with which, aided by the guilt of her evil intentions, he had no difficulty in making her glad to accept of the ornaments and fixtures left behind, (which, with the additional kitchen-furniture Miss St. Vincent had bought, could not have cost less than a hundred pounds, and were, in reality, worth seventy to the woman) as a full recompence for the thirty guineas due for rent. Thus did the

gene-

generous heart of Mr. Villiers punifh a wretch that I would have half hanged, by giving her as much more as was her due; but he confidered, that to pull and tear the things down, would render them of no more value than juft to pay the rent, he therefore chofe to let even an unworthy woman enjoy the benefit, rather than do mifchief for mifchief's fake.

C H A P. XII.

Mifs St. Vincent in continuation.

NOthing could have given more pleafure to Mifs St. Vincent than the fight of her old fervant at that critical juncture, but the poor

girl

girl was so shock'd at seeing such a change in so short a space, that she had much ado to support it; but, by a lucky presence of mind she got her emotions partly suppressed, lest it might affect her mistress, who seemed to want no additional distress, to assist a disorder that had made such visible progress in sapping the foundations of so precious a life: she therefore began to give her mistress an account how Mr. Villiers had found her, and in what manner he had brought away all her apparel, &c. adding, that she was sorry he had given the hard-hearted wretch so much for her rent; "and I "should have been sorry," says this amiable temper'd creature, "had he "given her less than her real due; "for her sordidness is no rule to a

"gene-

" generous bofom. But," fays fhe,
" where is this worthy creature?
" where is Mr. Villiers? tell him,"
added fhe, (guefling his motive for
ftaying away) " that my foul in his
" abfence wings its flight much fafter
" than when he is prefent; and if
" any thing could detain it here on
" earth, it would be a defire of giv-
" ing relief to an anxiety that I
" have had the misfortune to lodge
" in the bofom of the beft of men."
Mr. Villiers was juft opening the
door gently, when he heard her pro-
nounce thefe words; on which he
approached her foftly, and kneeling,
took her hand; " O lovely Maria,"
fays he, " can you wifh to relieve
" my anguifh, and not take the only
" method to do it, by ftriving to
" live?" " If my endeavouring to

" live,"

" live," says she, with a look of
ineffable goodness, " will alleviate
" your sorrows, be assur'd my ut-
" most efforts should not be want-
" ing; but the Almighty Ruler of
" this world has ordained it other-
" ways; I must therefore beg, that
" you will let the gentleman of the
" law draw a small writing to empow-
" er you not only to take care of my
" little effects, but to call the inhu-
" man wretch to account, who has
" thus cruelly destroy'd me. I think,
" if ever he returns to this country,
" although I would not touch his
" life, yet he ought not peaceably to
" enjoy the fruits of such cool, de-
" liberate villainy." " If, after the
" loss of my Maria, (which Heaven
" forbid)" says Mr. Villiers, " I
" should chance to survive, my only
                              " motive

" motive to endure life, will be to
" seek that wretch to the end of the
" world." " Why," says the lovely
sufferer, " will you dismiss my soul,
" disquieted within me, by the dread
" of involving a worthy man in a
" quarrel, with a wretch below his
" notice ? Promise me to leave him
" to the just laws of his country, and
" the stings of his own conscience,
" or you will load the few moments I
" have to breathe with more disquiet
" than any thing I have yet felt."
" I do; my ever adorable angel, I
" do" replies Mr. Villiers, " pro-
" mise, that I will obey your injunc-
" tions in every thing you wish."
On this the dear creature, with a
look of inexpressible complaisance,
murmured out, " I thank you;
" but where," says she, " is this
" friend of yours, the attorney ?"

Mr.

Mr. Villiers, knowing he was in the houfe, waiting to fee him again before he went away, fent for him into the room; he directly drew a little fketch of what fhe intended, which fhe figned, faying, " It is " needlefs to recommend my poor " fervants to your care." Then, as if fhe had no further ufe for life, fhe funk back in her chair, quite motionlefs; at that inftant the phyfician came in, he foon perceived the cold hand of death was on her, tho' he feem'd to think the inexorable tyrant had been more eager to fnatch his prey than he could poffibly have expected; but hearing what, at her earneft requeft, they had been doing, " I am not furprized then," fays he, " that the exertion of the fmall fhare " of fpirits fhe had left, has fhort-

" ened

" ened her precious life a few hours."
All this time Mr. Villiers was standing as immoveable and as senseless as a marble statue, holding her left hand in both his, whilst the Doctor was feeling for a pulse, and trying, with a polish'd glass, if she yet breath'd; when she once more open'd her lovely eyes, and fix'd them with a look of unspeakable tenderness for some moments on Mr. Villiers first; then cast them up to Heaven, and instantly closed them for ever. Thus fell, by the cruel hand of unrelenting man, an earthly seraphim, who, had she liv'd, would have been as much the ornament of her own sex, as the delight of ours.

Rest thy precious soul, says I; if my thin body could vye with the

clouds

clouds in shedding tears, I would exhauſt their fountains dry in bewailing thy loſs.

C H A P. XIII.

The author parted from Mr. Villiers.

I Have heard philoſophers aſſert, that extremes of ſudden joy are more dangerous than extremes of ſorrow; but here ſorrow proved fatal indeed; her delicate frame, nurs'd from a tender plant by the care of her worthy guardian, in a greenhouſe where the ſun eternally ſhone, ſhrunk beneath the bitter blaſt it was ſo ſuddenly expoſed to; ſhrunk, never to rear its beauteous head again. Death too greedily ſeized

that

that opportunity of laying its icy hand, and clapping the feal of eternal night upon fuch blooming merit.

Mr. Villiers had juft recovered fenfe enough to receive her laft glance, and fee her expire; which threw him not only back into a ftate of infenfibility, but feemed to threaten moft alarming effects; therefore his friend, Mr. Meanwell, judging that the fight of the dear object, to him and to the world for ever loft, would only ferve to increafe an emotion already grown too powerful for him to controul, ordered a chair directly, into which he was carried quite infenfible, and conveyed home, the good follicitor attending the fide of the chair all the way, and affifting his own fervant to keep him from falling off the feat; he was inftantly put to bed, where he lay three weeks before any judgment could be formed whether grief would not have a worfe effect on him than it even had on the poor departed angel, by depriving him of his fenfes; but nature at laft got the better, and his reafon began to return: the firft inftance he gave of it was his faying, " And why " would the ever lovely Maria die, " and leave me behind?" " Becaufe," fays Mr. Meanwell, " fhe left you " behind to call to a fevere account " the villain that murder'd her." " And, by Heavens, fo I will," fays he, making an effort to rife, but was fo enfeebled he was not able. " So you fhall," fays Mr. Meanwell, " but to accomplifh it, inftead of

" lament-

" lamenting what Heaven decreed,
" and therefore can't be recalled,
" you muſt endeavour to regain that
" health and vigour neceſſary to ac-
" compliſh your end, it being a taſk
" worthy your great foul."

Although the worthy Mr. Meanwell deſigned nothing but to drive
out one paſſion by ſubſtituting another, leſs dangerous, in its place, yet
I have reaſon to think, he unwarily
laid the foundation of a troubleſome
piece of work for Mr. Villiers;
who, now that reſentment ſupplied
the place of grief, recovered his
ſtrength amazingly faſt, and, in leſs
than a fortnight, was able to go a-
broad. Mr. Meanwell had taken
care to order a genteel funeral for
Miſs Vincent, at which her man and

maid

maid attended, and were, I believe, the moſt real mourners that have followed a hearſe in town for theſe fifty years paſt. The firſt thing Mr. Villiers did, was to order mourning for his dear loſt Maria; then ſending for the man and maid, he gave them all her cloaths, and one hundred pounds a-piece, reſerving her jewels as precious reliques, to be eternally preſerved in remembrance of her. Then took ſuch pains to write abroad, to enquire where the villain reſided; that in leſs than three months he heard the wretch was ſquandering the fruits of the dear lady's murder at Venice: thither he inſtantly prepared to follow him; but, unluckily, as he would not leave a ſingle debt unpaid, I was delivered, along with

some

some other notes, into the hands of the long-jaw'd undertaker, that had the gloomy pleasure (for pleasure it is to those people) of performing the last sad office, man could render to the departed saint.

Whether the Great Disposer of all things suffer'd Mr. Villiers to find the wretch, and make an example of him, or permitted him to drag on a life that must soon become a prey to poverty, infamy, and a guilty conscience, I know not, and therefore am as much unable to satisfy my reader's curiosity as my own; but of this, gentle reader, be assur'd, that although to our short-sighted intellects, the ways of Heaven seem dark and intricate, yet nothing is more certain than that an

uner-

unerring hand rules over all, and what ſeems to us partial evil, always tends to the general good.

C H A P. XIV.

Long faces not always ſure ſigns of grief.

MY laſt chapter ended with my falling into the hands of Mr. Longjaws the undertaker; away he walk'd home with me, another kind of a pace than his funeral-march, for now he not only trotted, but whiſtled all the way : his tune indeed was the Babes in the Wood, but that to him, I ſuppoſe, was a merry tune, becauſe it exhibited an idea of two buryings at once. When he came home,

home, he afk'd, "who had enquired
"for him?" "Sir," fays an odd looking fellow, with a phiz as dark as
the rufty black coat he had on, and
therefore qualified for a deep mourner,
"Mr. Ticktack the clockmaker's
"daughter is dead, and he has or-
"dered a handfome coffin with grey
"fuperfine and beft furniture." "Ve-
"ry well," fays Longjaws, raifing
the key of his tune, and giving an
additional fhake every other bar.
"And," fays the fellow, "the grocer's
"wife over the way can't live, fo he
"has befpoke a coffin, covered with
"fuperfine black." "Better ftill,"
fays Longjaws, fhaking the laft bar
of his tune fo long and fo loud, I
thought he defign'd to bring the top
of his fhop down. What a fellow is
here! thinks I; by his own good

will

will I find he would make no bones
of whistling all the world into the
church-yard, though he left nobody
to listen to the trill of his wind-
pipe but his own dear self.   I began
to wish myself out of his company,
for fear of his whistling me into
some church-yard or other; but fortune did not favour my wishes, till
I had done pennance with this master of ceremonies to the dead for
eight or ten days; during which
time, what with his whistling, and
what with that sable-fac'd journey-
man of his driving nails into coffins, I receiv'd such a shock in the
drum of my ears, that I lay three
days in the pocket of a woollen-
draper, to whom he paid me for
black and grey cloth, before the single vibration of a sound from his
lady's

lady's tongue, made the leaft impref-
fion on my auditory nerves; though,
by the motion of her lips, and the
ferenity of her countenance, I found
the honeft man had a hot difh of
Billingfgate every morning for breakfaft, over and above his curtain en-
tertainment in the night,

But before I part with mafter
Longjaws, I muft recount one ftory
about him, which happened the
day after I fell into his hands; had
it not happened fo foon, I could
have given no account at all of any
of his tranfactions, for my ears, that
very afternoon, and all the time I
ftaid with him afterwards, were fo
ftunn'd with his merry tune of the
Babes in the Wood, to which the
difmal fac'd fellow's hammer played
an

an excellent thorough-bafs on the heads of the brafs nails, that, as I told you before, my ears became as ufelefs to me, as learning to a pupil-monger. But to proceed.

CHAP. XV.

Long jaws continued.

THis genius of an undertaker, into whofe hands I was fallen, had another trade; for he was an upholfterer. When he buried a cuftomer, he was always looking out fharp, to furnifh a houfe for the heir; and, when he had fitted up a houfe, he then began to look fharp for a funeral; not regarding how foon he car-

carried them out of the house, to the church yard. Being one of what you call fore-right fellows, in conversation with his customers, he often jumbled the two trades strangely together. Going, the morning after, I fell into his hands, with a gentleman, to look at a house, which he had recommended to him. " Sir," says he, " I am sure you can't dislike this " house; I furnish'd it for the gen- " tleman that lived here last, and bu- " ried both him and all his family " out of it, and I hope I shall have " the honour of doing the same by " you and your family." The gentleman surveying the man from top to toe, as if he was measuring which was the biggest half of him, the knave or the fool, replied, with a smile, " But you'll stay till I am
" dead

" dead firſt?" " Certainly," ſays
the undertaker, not aware of the
archneſs with which the gentleman
ſpoke, " I am too good a Chriſtian
" to bury folks alive. I never did
" it in all my life, but once; it was
" poor Mrs. * * * *, and I told her
" huſband I thought ſhe was not
" dead·" " But" he ſaid, " did not
" he know her better than me?" ſo
" he made me ſcrew her down with, I
" believe, fifty ſcrews; he would
" not let me touch the coffin with a
" ſingle nail, for fear the hammer
" ſhould awake her: but, God for-
" give me, if I don't believe it was
" only a trance ſhe was in; but the
" job was a good job, and I had no
" buſineſs to interfere between man
" and wife, they two muſt have a
" reckoning ſome day or other about
" it,

" it, as fure as God is in Heaven ; but
" I wafh'd my hands of the matter, as
" foon as I had finifh'd. But I never
" fhall forget how faft I fcrew'd her
" down ; he faid fhe had been fo
" good a creature he could not
" take too much care the furgeons
" did not get her ; fo ordered the
" grave-digger half a crown to fill
" up her grave directly, and ram
" the ground well down." " For
" which reafon," fays the gentleman,
with the fame arch look and tone,
" if ever you bury my wife, that fhe
" may have fair play, you fhall nail
" her down." " And I can fecure
" her as well that way," replies the
unmeaning fellow, " as any under-
" taker in town can do with fix inch
" fcrews." On this the gentleman,
once more, took meafure of him
with

with his eye, fmiled, and departed;
and the undertaker whiftled his way
home, to prepare houfhold furniture and coffins for his new cuftomers.

I lay ten days in the woollen-dra-
per's pocket, during which time I
recovered part of of my hearing, in
fpite of madam's tongue, which,
though louder than the undertaker's
whiftle and hammer put together,
yet having only two hours of it in
the morning, I had all the reft of
the day, and all the night to recover
in, the curtain-lecture falling all to
her hufband's own fhare, for he left
me in his pocket below ftairs; fo
that I had recovered pretty tolerably,
when I was given in change to a
gentleman of fortune, who put me
into

into his little fob-pocket-book, and
away he drove to the Smyrna.
Whilſt he was ſipping his coffee, he,
as well as myſelf could not help liſtening to a gentleman, who kept
talking away to an old Captain that
did not return a ſingle word in anſwer; nor had he occaſion, for the
gentleman never made a moment's
pauſe, but kept going on as if he
did not value his words at above
four-pence a million, and, by the
ſample I heard, that was a very
good price for them. An acquaintance of my owner's, who ſat at the
ſame table, ſeeing him liſten and
ſtare, told him, the gentleman had
been talking an hour before he came
in, and he anſwered for it, it would
hold an hour longer, unleſs, by
good luck, he was engaged elſe-
where,

where, which, to the great relief of
the whole company, he luckily was ;
fo that after a further ftring of about
ten minutes long of words, (which
were all noun fubftantives, becaufe
having no connection with each
other, they were all obliged to ftand
by themfelves) he decamp'd, and
received the filent thanks of the
whole company for fhewing them
his back.

My owner's acquaintance perceiv-
ing an enquiring kind of curiofity
in his face, began thus :

" That gentleman, who talks fo
" much, and fays nothing, has per-
" haps better reafons for making
" ufe of unmeaning words than moft
" people imagine." " Reafons !"
fays

says my owner, "Can any man have
" a reason for wasting his words and
" time in saying nothing?" "Bless
" me," says my owner's friend,
" how little do you know of the
" matter? Did not Sir William
" Y——, in Sir Robert Walpole's
" time, obtain the post of secretary
" of war, for the sole qualification
" of talking two or three hours to-
" gether, without either himself, or
" any of the house being able to
" pick the least meaning out of a
" single sentence; and yet the lan-
" guage was very genteel and very
" polite? Is there not now a thou-
" sand men of great parts starving,
" whilst fellows that never were
" guilty of speaking a word of sense
" in their lives, occupy several con-
" siderable posts; but the gentleman

" just

"juſt now departed has better rea-
"ſons than all this; for at four years
"old he loſt a penſion by making
"a good ſpeech; he is at preſent in
"poſſeſſion of eight hundred a year,
"and his friends agree, nem. con.
"that he is in no danger of loſing
"it by ſuch an accident at preſent:
"but too much care cannot be taken
"in ſuch tickliſh affairs. I am
"therefore apt to think that he is
"ſome how or other always upon
"his guard, elſe, in ſpite of his
"teeth, he muſt once in ſeven years,
"amidſt an ocean of words, have
"blundered out one tolerable ſen-
"tence, which, I am really inform'd,
"has not really happened in that
"period." He then told my owner
the whole ſtory of the gentleman's
being ſo unlucky as to loſe his firſt

4   penſion

penſion at ſo early an age; all which I bottled up, and did not loſe a ſingle ſyllable; therefore, gentle reader, if you have curioſity enough to follow me through all the tranſactions that preceded, and occaſioned this unfortunate ſpeech, that loſt the four-years-old penſion, I'll tell you the ſtory; but you muſt have all the apparatus, for I never will lug in a tale by the head and ſhoulders, as Joe Miller, or ſome ſuch profound writer, tells us, a man did by Sampſon, for having no tale in his budget but one, which happened to be about this ſaid Sampſon, and being willing to club his ſtory with other people, let the ſubject be what it would, he always lugg'd in poor Sampſon, and thereby proved himſelf ſtronger than the

L 2   ſtrongeſt

ſtrongeſt man in the world. What
do you ſay to it, my gentle reader ?
I don't ſay readers, becauſe I would
not ſuppoſe you would cheat my
thrice-worthy friend the great cir-
culating librarian, by reading two
or three at a time in one and the
ſame book ; I therefore repeat, gentle reader, will you attend or not ?

I won't detain you long, like a
certain lawyer of whom I heard a
gentleman tell a ſtory, which I
ſhall firſt give you in his own words,
as nigh as I can remember.

" I was one day," ſays the
gentleman, " in Weſtminſter-hall,
" when a certain very eminent law-
" yer, on going to ſpeak, was two
" or three times interrupted, but at
" laſt

" laft he got his lordfhip's ear, and
" then began his fpeech: " My
" lord," fays he, " a—hem—I have
" very little to fay—hem—hem—I
" promife I fhall not detain the court
" long—hem—hem—hem—but it
" is hard to be interrupted, when
" what I have to fay will be faid in
" fo few words—hem—hem—hem
" —hem—very little explanation
" will make the court and the
" jury underftand the cafe as clear-
" ly to the full as I do myfelf, a
" —hem—a—hem—But, my lord,
" your lordfhip muft own, when a
" man has fo very little to fay, it
" is very hard he fhould be inter-
" rupted. It is not my talent to de-
" tain the court with long fpeeches,
" or go about and about with need-
" lefs circumlocutions to miflead the

L 3   " court

" court and the jury. I undertake
" to speak in no cause that needs
" the aid of such evasive doings; I
" love to come to the marrow, as I
" may say, of the bone at once,
" that the court and the jury may
" taste the merits of the cause at
" first setting out; this prevents
" their palates from being vitiated
" by false sauces, which will be pre-
" sented them in long artful speeches,
" wherein several of my brethren,
" both to the right and left, are
" adepts. I say, therefore, my lord,
" is it not hard that a man that has
" so little to say, should be so often
" interrupted. I complain of it,
" my lord, because it happens more
" frequently with me than any other
" practitioner at the bar; I never
" interrupt any gentleman; I never
" cut

" cut any body fhort, and give an an-
" fwer to what a gentleman is going
" to fay : I confine my anfwers to
" what a gentleman has faid, not
" what he is about to fay. I hear all
" with patience and attention, my
" lord; and, in the main, there is
" good policy in acting fo, if rightly
" confidered; for give people rope
" enough, and nine out of ten will
" hang themfelves; but if I indulge
" every man in his own, if I keep
" my eyes open either by treading
" on my own toes, or making me-
" morandums of my own private
" concerns, or by any other me-
" thods well known to the court;
" if I do all this, I fay, my lord,
" fhould not I have the fame indul-
" gence as other people? fauce
" for a goofe is fauce for a gander

" all

" all the world over, my lord; that
" proverb is admitted in every
" court in Europe; and three or four
" hundred years peaceable poffeffion,
" will furely prevent any ejectment
" from being brought againft that
" good old faying, my lord, and I
" claim the benefit of it: I fhall
" take up very little of your time, I
" affure your lordfhip."

" The learned counfellor's luckily
" mentioning fauce for a goofe, loft
" me the remainder of his preface,
" which did not, I am told, laft a-
" bove an hour longer, and, by that
" time, he had forgot his fhort
" fpeech, and never came at the
" marrow of his marrow-bone; but I,
" at the found of the word *goofe*,
" recollected I was to dine that day
" on

" on a fine goofe, on which I afk'd
" a manly looking gentleman that
" ftood clofe befide me, in a white
" curl'd wig, and feemed, to my
" thinking, to be a mafter-taylor,
" if he could tell me what o'clock
" it was? he inftantly pulled out a
" gold watch, with a chain of five
" links, and two feals dangling at
" the end of each link. I then con-
" cluded he was a toyman, and took
" that genteel method of carrying
" part of his fhop about him;
" finding by the information of this
" gentleman's ten-fealed watch, that
" I fhould, by putting the beft leg
" foremoft, be fcarce able to arrive
" time enough to cut up the goofe,
" which is an exercife I take great
" delight in, efpecially if it is a fat
" one, I therefore abruptly left the

learned

" learned man of the law convin-
" cing the judge what a fhort fpace
" of his time he would encroach
" upon, and haftened to get a leg
" and a wing, and, perhaps, a fmall
" flice on the breaft, of what would
" be of more fervice to me than
" all the appurtenances of the law
" put together, which, I am told,
" in this kingdom amount to the
" fmall number of fourfcore thou-
" fand fouls."

Are not you very glad, gentle
reader, that the gentleman got his
belly full of goofe, inftead of ftaying
for the remainder of the lawyer's
fpeech? I am, I affure you; it could
have been of no fervice to any body
but my bookfeller; for as I never
curtail any body's fpeeches, you muft
have

have had thirty pages more, either
to have read or fkipp'd over, before
we had come to this unfortunate,
fenfible, four-year-old fpeech of
Dickey's, which, at fo early an age,
loft him a penfion; but now, thanks
to the goofe and the gander, we fhall
come at it in good time.

" You muft know," fays my owner's friend, " that this gentleman's
" name is Richard, (though there
" was no faint of that name, yet fe-
" veral good men, to my knowledge,
" have been called Richard before
" now; king Richard's name was
" Richard, but as I can't fay much
" for him, I'll proceed :) now as this
" gentleman's name is Richard, they
" therefore, when a boy, called him
" Dickey. Dickey, though he is grown
                                " up

" up to be Richard, and hopes to be
" Sir Richard some day, when the
" fit takes the king to knight a few
" calves, loves to hear it mention'd
" that he once said a good thing,
" and therefore never fails to tell the
" tale himself, though to nobody
" but friends and strangers, but
" Dickey, (Richard, I should have
" said, now he is a man) has the art
" of flattening a story so much,
" that people can't tell when he has
" finished; whether he begun with
" the good thing or ended with it, or
" wrapp'd it up in the middle of his
" tale, but take it upon trust that
" it was somewhere in the story, tho'
" they could not clearly espy the
" place."

Methinks

Methinks I hear a lion-faced fellow, whofe two principal fangs are changed into two broken black ftumps, bawl out, Hold, fir, if you thus interrupt yourfelf, you'll never get on with your ftory. My grim looking friend, no matter for that; if I get on with my book 'tis the fame thing to me; my bookfeller pays me by the fheet, and the reader can but have his meafure; a belly full is a belly full, though it be only of that kind of Irifh wall-fruit call'd potatoes, but rather than difturb the harmony of your features by making you angry, I'll proceed with all imaginable expedition, though, in fpite of the fierceft face you can put on, I'll end this chapter firft.

CHAP.

CHAP. XVI.

Much ado about what is worſe than nothing.

"Dickey's grandmother was a
"fine old lady, and valued
"herſelf greatly upon her delicacy.
"Unfortunately for her ſhe happen-
"ed to be ſtrangely troubled with a
"diſtemper, called by the ancient
"Saxons, the ghormhaarhuttles,
"but, by the learned diſciples of Ga-
"len, it is now called the wind-
"colic, which was not content with
"walking out at the fore-door of
"the old lady's clay tenement, with
"a guggling kind of a noiſe, called
"by the Froglanders, belchabacum-
"ſhau,

" fhau, but it would frequently if-
"fue out at a poftern-gate, with a
" noife like a crack'd trumpet,
" which would often fo embarrafs the
" the good old foul, that it put her
" upon ways and means of prevent-
" ing the confufion fhe was too often
" involved in, on account of thefe
" trumpet-like founds. Now this
" four-year-old Dickey being a fine
" hopeful boy, the grandmother de-
" clared him her favourite, and al-
" ways kept him clofe to her elbow,
" having previoufly agreed to give
" young Dickey a penny a day, to
" buy gingerbread with; for which
" it was ftipulated, that when any
" of thefe crack'd blafts happened,
" the old lady was to give him a rap
" on the pate, and fay, firrah, how
" dare you f—t fo? and Dickey
                              " was

" was to anfwer, I could not help it,
" grandmamma. Now one unfor-
" tunate day, a woeful day, a day
" indeed of woe; when Partridge's
" whole collection of evil ftars and
" planets had met, and clubb'd their
" heads together, how to fhed their
" malign influence on the poor
" harmlefs old lady Dickey's grand-
" mamma, a large company of
" polite acquaintance were affem-
" bled at her houfe : whether the
" influence of thefe evil ftars rari-
" fied the air too much in the old
" lady's bowels, or from what other
" caufe it proceeded, I am not duly
" authorized to fay; but certain it
" is this Saxon diftemper, this ghorm-
" hanrhuttles became exceeding trou-
" blefome, and at the fame time fo
" bafhful before company, that it
" refufed

6

" refufed to come out at the fore-
" door, but thought to fneak away
" backwards in filence, which it did
" four or five times, but left fuch
" a perfume, that all the poor in-
" nocent dogs in the room got
" turned out. The old lady finding
" that fcheme would hold water no
" longer, boldly fent her gueft forth
" at the poftern-door, with the old
" trumpet-like found, and lent Dickey
" a rap, who replied, " I could not
" help it, grandmamma;" but on
" repeating it half a dozen times,
" fhe was obliged to feem more and
" more angry with her favourite
" Dickey, and, to all appearance,
" increafe the fmartnefs of her raps.
" Five times did this paragon of a
" boy, this four-year-old Dickey,
" bear the raps patiently, and an-

" fwer very properly; but the fixth
" time the old lady's knuckles
" chanc'd to hit fo hard, that they
" drove all patience out of Dickey's
" head, and before fhe could think
" what he was about, to her ever-
" lafting confufion he had utter'd
" the following fentence: " If you
" hit fo hard, grandmamma, I will
" not father your f—s any longer."
" Well might Dickey value himfelf
" upon this fpeech, for neither De-
" mofthenes or Cicero I am certain,
" in ten of the beft orations they
" ever fpoke in their lives, could
" excite fuch different fenfations in
" an audience, as this fingle fentence
" of Dickey's did: the delicate old
" lady, the grandmamma, turned
" pale, and was ready to fink thro'
" the fattin-cufhion that had fo often
                    " vibrated

1

" vibrated with thofe trumpet-like
" tones ; diftrefs appeared in the
" face of the old lady's daughter,
" Dickey's mamma ; mifs Squeam-
" ifh, the old maid, who, although
" fhe was near fifty, never had any
" more than one child, and two mif-
" carriages, fcrew'd up her face, and
" and look'd as if fhe had drank falt-
" water, and was going to throw it up
" again ; lady Lazarus———, whofe
" fore legs fhe fancied were a pro-
" found fecret, look'd fneeringly with
" a haughty difdain on a creature fub-
" ject to fuch a filthy diforder ; Mrs.
" Frowfey, whofe fkin had the na-
" tural perfume of tanner's-bark,
" kept opening and fhutting her
" gold-fnuff box, with fuch an air
" of delicacy, you would fwear fhe
" fed on nothing but ambrofia, and

M 2 " wafh'd

" wafh'd her hands in nectar inftead
" of perfumed pearl-powder, which,
" though laid on very thick, could
" not prevent the effluvia of her fkin
" from faluting your nofe : two or
" three ladies, by checking a laugh
" which had got half way out, put
" their faces into the attitude of a
" boy, whofe companion having
" given him a fmart ftroke with a
" fwitch, ftands confidering whether
" to laugh or cry. Lady Nicenofe,
" who has been known to fpend an
" hour at a time in the ftable with
" her hufband's coachman, (who is
" the dirtieft dog in the creation,
" and keeps both his ftable and
" horfes in as dirty a pickle as him-
" felf,) fainted at the thoughts of
" fitting in a room where fuch inde-
" licate fumes had mix'd with the
" pure

" pure air; whilſt the worthy, open-
" hearted lady Meanwell laugh'd her
" ſides almoſt ſore, and then, very
" ſenſibly obſerv'd, that although no-
" body was a greater friend to de-
" cency than herſelf, yet ſhe de-
" ſpiſed an over-affected nicety; for
" experience, ſhe was certain, would
" convince every one, whoſe life
" Providence ſhould be pleaſed to
" prolong, that old age was ſubject
" to infirmities which youth had no
" idea of, and nobody need be a-
" ſhamed of it, but thoſe who were
" aſhamed of being old: in ſhort,
" the good ſenſe of that lady,
" brought all the company to them-
" ſelves again, (except the coach-
" man's lady, by which I concluded,
" nothing but the ſmell of the ſta-
" ble would go down with her,) and

" Dickey

" Dickey was pronounced a very
" fine boy. But from that day
" he loft his penfion; whether it
" was the effect of a fudden ana-
" thema that might fecretly efcape
" from the old lady in the firft
" onfet of her confufion, or fome of
" the evil ftars fhed their bane-
" ful influence on Dickey's head,
" I know not, but certain it is, he
" never faid a good thing fince, nor
" ever will, if he lives to the age of
" old Parr."

Methinks I now hear another of
my wife-phizz'd readers fay, What
a long Canterbury-tale has this fellow built upon a f——! Your obfer-
vation, my worthy friend, is a very
juft one; but as the foundation of
my tale is ftronger than you are a-
ware of, I can't do lefs than pre-

sent it you to build a better tale
upon; if you can't do it, 'tis your
fault, not mine.

CHAP. XVII.

No good ever attends interruptions.

NEVER did I pass an afternoon so pleasantly in my life;
a dialogue betwixt lord George and
lady Mary, was maintained with
such true sense, spirit and delicacy,
and in so elegant a stile, that I am
very angry with myself for not being able to give my reader a faint
idea of it. The manners of high-
life, when guided by sense and in-
nate goodness of heart are truly ami-

M 4   able,

able, and the charming pair, (between whom this afternoon's conference was a cour:ſhip on my lord's ſide, and a half aſſent on the lady's,) vy'd with each other in delicacy of ſentiment and of expreſſion.

Lady Mary's grandmamma was preſent all the time, and a fine old lady ſhe is of her age as any in the four quality-pariſhes of St. James's, St. Martin's, St. George's, or Maryle-bone; yet although this match was as good as made up, you'll be ſurprized to think how ſlight an accident had like to have broke it off: but I'll tell you the ſtory.

I wiſh you would tell us firſt, ſays a ſea-captain, with a great cockade in his hat, how the devil you

you came into company with my
lord George, and lady Mary, and her
grandmother ? you talk of a fellow
bringing in Sampſon by the head
and ſhoulders, but if you have not
thruſt yourſelf into lord George's
and lady Mary's company by the
head and ſhoulders, I'll be d———d.

Noble captain, ſays I, don't be
in ſuch a paſſion ; you may be d——d,
for aught I know, whether I got in
by the head and ſhoulders, or heels
foremoſt ; but there I did get ; and
becauſe you have not aſk'd me ci-
villy, I won't tell you which way ;
therefore, if you don't chuſe to
hear the ſtory, you are welcome to
ſheer off.

What between ſea-calves and land-
lubbers, never was poor devil ſo
inter-

interrupted in his bufinefs as I am; this water-animal has driven all ideas fo totally out of my head, that I fhall never be able to put the ftory again into that pretty, nice roundeau that I had once fhap'd it. The fpirit of it is gone, and if I had not promifed it, my readers fhould not have been troubled with it; but if I muft come to difgrace, I rather chufe to do it by keeping my word than breaking it.

On Thurfday afternoon; of all days in the year, I think it was on a Thurfday; no, I am wrong;— it was Friday;—I am wrong again; it could not be Friday, becaufe I am fure it was not fo nigh the end of the week, and yet it was not Wednefday.—You muft excufe me, kind

kind reader, I am not recovered enough from the trepidation into which that captain with his greafy uniform put me, to tell this story as it ought to be told: fpare me a little, and I fhall recover by degrees, but if I clofe the chapter firft, you will have a better chance of knowing what I am about, becaufe I can take a fhort walk up and down my garret, to bring my fenfes about me before I begin again.

CHAP.

CHAP. XVIII.

The author escapes a scowering.

YOU must know, reader, that this same lord George is as complete a gentleman as ever entered a drawing-room; and lady Mary not a jot inferior in every qualification desireable in the fair sex; therefore to repeat a conversation, and do justice to this charming couple, requires a cool moment or two, for it ought not to be rabbled over like Mr. * * * *'s tales of cocks and bulls, which never reach the seat of the memory, but glance plump from the drum of the ear through

the

the noftrils, and mix with the open
air again in an inftant : for all which
caufes and confiderations I muft, my
thrice worthy reader, (I wifh I could
add, and admirer) beg you'll excufe
me entering upon that tafk for the
prefent, and I'll give you another
ftory that fhall begin with a lord.
But as he faid nothing, I fhall have
no converfation to repeat, but only
plain facts to relate, which I can ftill
do, in fpite of that captain's bluff
face and great cockade : but let me
firft premife, that I am not fo great
a coward as to be frightened by his
fierce looks and great cockade alone;
no, no; there was a farther confi-
deration, I was afraid he had a prefs-
warrant in his pocket; and all prefs-
warrants impower people to take
men in either ragged or thread-bare

coats

coats with impunity, becaufe they
are fure the poor wretches have no
friends to call them to account.

I was paid into the hands of a
noble lord, who rammed me, and
feveral more of my brethren, into
his waiftcoat-pocket in fuch a crump-
led condition, that I expected we
were, whenever the fit took him, to
be made ufe of at the temple of the
goddefs Cloacina; but the man had
more wit in his anger (as country-
folks fay); he carried us to Boodle's,
where he loft me at the firft bett,
and threw me a crofs the table to a
fober, careful-looking gentleman, (or
lord, or fomething or other, for he
muft be fomebody, or he would
hardly have been there) who un-
twifted me with great care, and put
me

me into his pocket-book, with as
much form as if he had been an honeſt money lending city uſurer. I
thought myſelf exceeding lucky, for
had my lord Harebrains offered to
untwiſt me, I ſhould have been torn
half in two, at leaſt, and then have
been glad to wear a ſtrengthening-
plaſter on my back all my life after. In this pious-fac'd gentleman's
pocket-book I lay very ſecure, but
in great fear of ſoon being taken out
again, and kick'd about from one
wild ſhaver to another, by which
means I ſhould have ſtood a chance,
in ſome angry fit or other, to get a
hole made in my body with their
nails, or a piece bit out of my ſides;
but my new maſter luckily proved a
gatherer, not a ſquanderer. Every
five minutes I had a freſh companion
coming

coming to take a nap in the pocket-
book. At laſt, juſt at the cloſe of
the evening, my maſter, who I ſhall
call Mynheer Van Steadyphiz, opened his pocket-book, and began to
examine his notes one by one, till
he came to me, and brought me as
carefully out as he had put me in;
ſure, thinks I, he has not loſt a
bett! however, as it is the firſt to-
night, he may well afford it; but I
ſoon found he was only giving a
young ſpark change for a note of a
hundred, having won eighty of him;
I was clapp'd into a little fob-pocket-book of the young gentleman's,
with nothing but a ſolitary fifty to
bear me company. I never paſſed
an evening ſo pleaſantly in my life;
he proved to be one of your ſenſible,
obſervation making notes, which I
did

did not wonder at, when he told me his father was an Eaſt-India Director, All the time our new maſter lay ſnoring, with as much content as if he had won five thouſand, inſtead of loſing one, we had a moſt agreeable chit-chat, and he told me ſeveral tales ; which, if I have time, the world ſhall be the better for, but not till I have unladed my own cargo. Little did I think that agreeable night would be attended with ſuch a tragical ſcene as it was in the morning, when I loſt, for ever loſt, my ſenſible friend, without hopes of ever ſeeing him again. I am ſure it has made ſuch an impreſſion on my ſpirits, that I cannot help wiſhing all your ſaucy common low-lived huſſies were ſent to Bridewell, and their keepers to Bedlam.

Our young master no sooner got
dress'd, than, to comfort himself
after his loss, away he went to
breakfast with his madam, a young
lady, whose mother had been so
great a friend to the butchers of
Clare-Market, that she had kindly
taken uncommon pains to convey
large quantities of beef, mutton,
veal, pork, &c. &c. from their shops
to the pot and spit: whether, like
Mr. Ashley, she did it *pro bono publico*, or like Mr. W—s, *pro patria*,
or like ✱ ✱ ✱ ✱, *pro rege*, I won't pretend to determine; all I can aver
with certainty is, that immense quantities she had conveyed in her time
from the market to the porrage-pot,
and had begun to initiate her daughter into the same trade, or mystery;
but the young lady, at the age of
thir-

thirteen, thought fit to give the preference to a more public occupation;
though, I believe, the firſt four
years of her labours, inſtead of prov-
ing *pro bono publico*, proved *pro bono
chirurgiano*. One of that profeſſion, to
whom ſhe had ſent a number of cuſtomers to get the bridges of their
noſes rectified, had the gratitude to
ſet her on her legs again, when ſhe
was either at, or very near the laſt
ſtage. Some folks are ſo ill-natur'd
as to think there was not ſo much
of gratitude in the act, as hopes of a
freſh harveſt from her induſtry, when
her conſtitution was ſtrong enough
to communicate that fatal diſeaſe a-
gain to her cuſtomers, without im-
pairing her external charms : but if
that was really the caſe, the noſe-
mender was bit, for juſt at the

time

time she was prepared and fitted for another cruise, our young hero took a fancy to her, hired her a house, and gave her fine cloaths, which enabled her (though she still followed her public business) to take her choice of culls so well, as to escape the dreadful distemper she had suffered so much from in the four first years of her beginning business.

My possessor—on his first coming into her breakfast-room, began to toy with her, but she put him off, and directly sat down to breakfast. I knew so much of those sort of cattle as to be sensible there must be something in the wind, when they refuse to perform the mysteries of their calling. I was not wrong in

my

my conjecture, for whilst the second dish of tea was pouring
out, " My dear," says she, " I want
" money." Ho! ho! thinks I, the
cat is out of the bag now ; ten to
one but before night I go again into
Taviftock-ftreet, and, perhaps, may
fee the black ftumps of my old acquaintance, Mrs. Doubleftitch again;
but I had reafon to be well-pleafed
that I never gueffed wider of the
mark in my life, for inftead of me
he lugg'd out my brother fifty, and
put him into her hands. Madam,
with an air of vulgarity which never
entirely quits perfons of her rank
and education, cries, " Fifty! and
" be d——d! why it will hardly
" ferve for a breakfaft." Then, to
make her words good, fhe clapped
my unfortunate comrade between

two

two flices of bread and butter, and
fwallowed him down with as much
agility as fhe had formerly taken
her pills and bolufes. Never was
aftonifhment equal to mine, all the
blood in my veins grew chill with
horror; and, had any body feen me,
I imagine I cut much the fame figure that Ulyffes did in the cave
of Polypheme, when he faw his
companions devoured by that one-
ey'd monfter. To fay truth, the aftonifhment of my owner was little
inferior to mine: like a cat watching a moufe, he kept ftaring at her
for at leaft two minutes, without
fuffering his eye-lids to make one
fingle wink. At laft, in the mild,
eafy, genteel tone, which fhe had
learned in the market, fhe began
thus : " Blaft your peepers, you fon
of

" of a w——e ; how dare you ufe
" me fo?" This pretty, eloquent,
little, fhort fpeech brought him out
of his reverie ; but, fomehow or o-
ther, infpired him with an inclination to imitate the fame ftile. Mifs
was partly out of luck with her airs
this time ; for he being rather fore
with his laft night's lofs, and fifty
going fo fuddenly without either
rhyme or reafon, brought all his
choler to his affiftance ; he firft flung
his own difh of fcalding-hot tea in
her face, by way of wafhing his
bank-note down, and then, in imi-
tation of her ftile I fuppofe, replied, " Blaft your eyes, you brim-
" ftone-whore, this is the laft penny
" you fhall ever have of mine." On
which, taking his hat, he walked
directly out of the houfe, before ma-

dam

dam had time to fall into a fit, which I obſerved ſhe was putting her face in tune to do, as ſoon as ſhe felt the warmth of the tea. I was congratulating my poſſeſſor on the conqueſt he had gained, and, at the ſame time, wiſhing the improvident wretch might never touch another penny, or even recover ſixpence of it from the Bank, till poverty had ſo waſted all the fleſh from her rump, that every director, if he choſe to peep, might plainly read the number on her hucklebone.

Whilſt I was buſy in theſe cogitations, her hopeful maid came running after us, bawling, " Sir, Sir! " dear Sir, my miſtreſs is dead." " Dead!" ſays my poſſeſſor, (who, from this time I call 'ſquire Shallow-crown,)

crown,) "why I left her alive but "juft now." "Very true, Sir," fays the girl, "but the inftant you ftep-"ped out of the door, fhe fell upon "the floor as flat as a flounder, and "is, by this time, I'll anfwer for it, "as ftiff as a poker; fhe juft had "had time to fay, O Betty, he's "gone, and my heart is broken." At this poor Shallowcrown began to melt like a tallow-candle, when there is a thief in it. "Betty" fays he, "do you think there is no hopes "of her recovery?" "Very little, "I fear, Sir; if your rubbing her "temples don't do it, there is fmall "chance indeed; but pray don't let "the poor creature be loft, becaufe "a poor woman can't help being "foolifh fometimes." "She fhan't, "if I can prevent it," fays Shallow-

crown;

crown; fo away he turns back. All this time I faw her peeping through a corner of her dining-room window, to fee how Betty fucceeded, that fhe might be dead or alive at her return, juft as the exigency of affairs required. I was therefore certain we fhould find her ftretch'd on the floor as dead as a herring. O man! man! thinks I, what fort of a ftrange animal art thou? An Englifh maftiff that fhuts both his eyes and runs plump into the gripe of a bear, is a prince of a dog for forefight, when compared to a muddy-brain'd two-legg'd puppy.

When we arrived at the habitation of this wretch, we found her juft as I expected, ftretched on the carpet with her petticoats fo neatly dif-diſpoſed, that they ſhew'd one of her legs to great advantage; and being a very fine limb'd brim, ſhe gueſs'd that would have *no* bad effect: the maid inſtantly fell to roaring and bawling, and calling for cold water and hartſhorn, whilſt my friend Timothy Shallowcrown ſat down on the carpet, and taking her head on his lap, fell to chafing her temples; but he chaf'd, and Betty flung water in her face for five minutes all in vain; ſhe, like Sidrophel, when he bit both Hudibras and Ralpho,

Shut both her eyes, and held her breath,
And to the life out-acted death.

How nature could, in one creature, make ſuch a ſtrange mixture of deep cunning and abſurdity, I ſhould
be

be at a loss to account, did I not see
instances of it every day both in man
and woman : instances so contra-
dictory, that what my eyes really behold, I can scarce reconcile myself
believe.—When madam had kick'd
and sprawl'd about, with as much
art as if she had been seven years
apprentice to the trade, she at last
came to life again ; (I fancy all my
readers guess she intended it from
the first,) when staring wildly at master Shallowcrown, just as you have
seen Juliet do at her beloved Romeo,
she suddenly seiz'd him round the
neck, and, in the tragical tone ex-
claim'd, " And art thou returned ?
" Never, O never will we part again."
" No; no more we will, Polly,"
says Shallowcrown ; this he spoke so
like Jubilee Dickey, that, in spite

of

of all my anger, it fet me a laughing heartily. However, to make fhort of my long ftory, which begins to tire myfelf as well as my readers, before any other bufinefs could be entered upon, fhe made him give her a draught on his banker for two hundred pounds; and, on fearching his pocket-book, condefcended to take poor me to buy ribbands with. Adieu, fays I to my quondam mafter, as he went out at the door, thou art a gudgeon of the firft clafs; rather than not be taken, I find thou wilt fwallow the naked hook; and if this moft abandon'd, unthinking wretch doth not bring thee to a morfel of bread, I'll give thee leave to fay when I am dead, that Solomon, the wifeft man in the world, and myfelf the moft learned

of

of bank-notes, were only a brace of buzzards.

I did not remain long with this Mrs. Mac Devil, which pleafed me not a little; for befides being in danger of walking down her wide throat, (where I fhould have cut a fmall figure, her paffage having admitted a fifty-pounder before,) I did not like her company, as I was fure not one of her actions would be worth remembering, unlefs the curfe of poverty had fallen upon her, which could not be, fo long as I ftaid with her; I was therefore glad to go, and will tell you how I went, and why, and wherefore.

After the maid and her brimfhip had diverted themfelves with the moft vulgar

vulgar cutting jokes and sneers upon this master Toby Shallowcrown, which I own he richly deserv'd, altho' from her it was the blackest ingratitude, Mrs. Abigail suddenly recollected that she had struck the finishing-stroke in fetching him back, and therefore deserved a new gown, at least, for her trouble; so told her mistress she could not give her less than five guineas to buy a silk gown with: for my part I thought the wench mighty reasonable in her demands; she displayed great generalship in persuading him to return; and uncommon presence of mind all the time her mistress's hum-cull fit lasted. But here behold another instance of the most absurd inconsistency; this wretch, who could so wantonly destroy such a sum as fifty pounds

6

pounds for nothing but a certainty of doing njury to the man from whom fhe received her daily bread, all on a fudden now becomes covetous, becaufe called upon to gratify a perfon that really deferved ten times more than fhe afk'd ; for had mafter Toby Shallowcrown gotten fairly away in his paffion, the odds would have been greatly againft Mifs Brim, whether fhe would ever have feen him again; notwithftanding which, fhe flatly refus'd the five guineas, and the mild Mrs. Abigail as ftoutly infifted upon it : this brought on a fcene of altercation, attended with a whole cart-load of accufations and recriminations, uttered in fuch an amazing, uncommon ftile, that all the converfation-pieces of St. Giles's, Chick-Lane, Hockley-

Hockley in the Hole, Billingſgate, nay, even Newgate itſelf, would appear the eſſence of polite converſation, compared to this Tartarian dialogue. At laſt the maid, with a volley of imprecations, ſuch as would have frightened the devil himſelf away, had he been liſtening, ſwore that ſhe would inſtantly find out Shallowcrown, and blow her miſtreſs to hell; I aſk pardon for uſing the mild Mrs. Abigail's own words, but I could not help thinking them very expreſſive.

The Abigail's laſt ſentence utter'd with a determin'd air, inſtantly brought Miſs Brim to her ſenſes: ſhe found ſhe had met with her match, ſo was forc'd to come down ten guineas inſtead of five, on which I was directly sent to the tea-shop for a pound of tea and change.

Thus was I delivered out of the hands of a fiend, with the most heavenly person joined to the most hellish tongue and rotten heart of any human being that, I believe, ever was, or ever will be created.

Would you reflect, O ye simple youths, what wretches you foster in your breasts, what vipers you warm in your bosoms; instead of suffering your deluded senses to be drawn away by painted sepulchres, filled with rottenness, you would view them with horror and detestation, and, in spite of all the efforts of ungovernable lust, sicken at the thoughts of embracing such ma-

gazines

6

gazines of corruption. But I am a-
afraid I am preaching to the wind,
or, at leaft, fhall have no better
fuccefs than an honeft ale-drinking
parfon, not above fifteen miles from
town, who, every Sunday morning,
mounts his pulpit with a defign to
awake his parifhioners to a due fenfe
of their fins, inftead of which, as
fure as he mounts, he preaches them
all faft afleep.

C H A P. XIX.

*Contains nothing but a Jew, a leg of
pork, and a peafe-pudding.*

THE laft chapter left me in the
hands of the tea-man, but this
chapter won't find me there for all
that, becaufe I was inftantly paid

ʃto

to a tea-broker, who carried me directly into the city, and delivered me into the hands of the ugliest dog of a Jew that the fun ever fhone upon. With this Ifraelite I went home to dinner, pleafed with an opportunity of feeing how thefe quondam people of God, far'd now-a-days. I expected, by the appearance of this Achan—the fon of Zerah*—that I fhould fee him fit down to a head of garlick, with a piece of bread and falt, and, perhaps, a fallad ; for all the cloaths on

---

* The 22d chapter of Jofhua, verfe 20. Did not Achan the fon of Zerah commit a trefpafs in the accurfed thing, and wrath fell on all the congregation of Ifrael.

N. B. Our author puts down this note to fhew, that he feldom gives folks names without a meaning.

his

his back were not worth above nine-
pence, on a moderate calculation; but
how was I furprifed to fee a fine leg
of pork and a peafe pudding come
fmoaking upon table; the Hebrew,
without a fingle ejaculation, or fo
much as lifting up his eyes, fell at
the pork with fuch eagernefs, that I
expected he would not fo much as
leave the fhank unfwallowed; but I
was miftaken, for I believe four
pounds was the moft he did eat, (the
leg weighed eight) but the pudding
paid very feverely for his mercy
to the pork; for although he left
very near half the leg of the forbid-
den beaft, yet not a tenth part of
the pudding efcaped the rage of his
grinders; the moment the act of
maftication ceafed, he feized on
a two-handled cup, much fuch a one

O 3   as

as Homer deſcribes old Neſtor's, and clapping it with both hands to his greaſy thick lips, took a moſt unchriſtian-like ſwig, but what the liquor was I had no time to enquire, for the inſtant he had finiſhed, he wiped his mouth with the back of his hand, where he let both the wet and greaſe remain to dry, and ran away directly to carry me to a poor needy ſhopkeeper, who not only paid him a guinea for a month's loan of me, but was at the charge of ſend-ing cloth of twice the value to the Iſraelite's warehouſe to lay as ſecurity.

The ſhopkeeper did not keep me a moment, but ran like bewitched to take up a bill that lay at a banker's.

CHAP.

CHAP. XX.

By which the reader may judge how ma-
ny feet a Spaniard takes at a stride.

BY the banker I was paid next
morning to a tradesman, who
kept grumbling at my Lord Four-
eyes, for ordering his goods out of
his shop without ever intending to
pay for them, and pondering to himself what name was bad enough for
him: honest man, thinks I, call him
a thief at once.

For my part I never had any great
notion of noble blood running in any
man's veins: where the pox must he
get it; can the king, by making a

man

man a peer, transfuſe noble blood
into the grandſon of a low uſurer?
ridiculous!

This puts me in mind of a dialogue I heard my father read between
a poor Spaniſh nobleman and a rich
gentleman, who would have married
his daughter, and kept both her and
her father and mother in affluence;
but tho' reduc'd to a cruſt, and that
cruſt not to be come at above three
days a-week, yet the noble Don kept
up his part.

"It was one of my anceſtors," ſays
this Don Furioſo del Meagrephizo,
(meaſuring at the ſame time the
whole length of a thirty foot room
at ſix ſtrides, and continuing to do
it backward and forward all the
time

time he was fpeaking,) " that banifh-
" ed the fun from his prefence for
" ever, for daring to fhine on that
" infamous day, when a petty gen-
" tleman of Andalufia was made a
" grandee of Spain; and fhall I, the
" defcendant in a direct line from
" fuch a heroe as that, difgrace fo
" illuftrious a race by matching my
" daughter below her dignity? for-
" bid it all the fhades of my noble
" anceftors!"

" The noble fhades of your an-
" ceftors, (fays the gentleman,) may
" with great propriety forbid it, be-
" caufe they can live upon air: but
" can they bid, as well as forbid?"

" Bid what?" fays the Don.

" Why, bid you," replies the gentleman, " to a good dinner and
" fupper; which I can, and will do
" every

" every day ; and, by producing a
" fat furloin of beef, or a well-fed
" turkey, do more than all your great
" anceftors put together can. But
" pray how far back do you go for
" your anceftors ?"

Don. " To the great Romulus the
" founder of Rome."

Gent. " And pray who was that
" Romulus ?"

Don. " I told you, the founder of
" Rome."

Gent. " True, you did ; but was
" he nothing elfe ?"

Don. " Yes ; he was the greateft
" man in the then known world."

Gent. " The greateft rogue you
" mean ; and could the people he
" fled from have catched him, they
" would have branded him on the
" back, and chained him to an oar :
" but

" but he had the forefight to join
" with a gang of thieves and vaga-
" bonds, the fcum of all the nations
" round them; numbers made them
" ftrong enough to defend them-
" felves at firft, and defpair prefent-
" ly rendered them fo formidable,
" that they called themfelves heroes;
" and from this neft of murderers,
" pirates, rogues, and pickpockets,
" the dregs of nations, and the
" outcafts of the world, the great
" families of the Italian Signores,
" the Spanifh Dons, the German
" princes; the French monfeigneurs,
" and the Englifh dukes and earls
" are all defcended: for fhame! for
" fhame! talk to fools and idiots
" of noble ideas by inheritance:
" where was the nobility of the firft
" man? Mr. Adam was a noble gar-
" dener, and earned his living by the
" fweat

" fweat of his brow. Did he dig
" the noble blood he tranfmitted to
" part of his pofterity out of the
" earth, or where elfe could he firft
" find it, think you ?"

Whether the Don liften'd to the
voice of reafon, joined with the crav-
ings of an empty ftomach, or that
pride prevailed, and kept him ftrut-
ting with empty pockets up and
down his empty room, I cannot inform you, becaufe the fheet of paper in which my father had brought
a-quarter of a pound of butter from
the chandler's fhop, ended where I
do ; and as I fcorn to coin either a
beginning or ending for my own true
tales, you may be fure I will not do
it for any body elfe.

END OF THE THIRD VOLUME.

Lightning Source UK Ltd.
Milton Keynes UK
UKHW030154240223
417572UK00008B/486